The Hamlet Vocation of Coleridge and Wordsworth

MARTIN GREENBERG

The Hamlet Vocation

OF COLERIDGE

AND WORDSWORTH

UNIVERSITY OF IOWA PRESS IOWA CITY

University of Iowa Press, Iowa City 52242
Copyright © 1986 by the University of Iowa
All rights reserved
Printed in the United States of America
First edition, 1986

Jacket and book design by Sandra Strother Hudson
Typesetting by G&S Typesetters, Inc., Austin, Texas
Printing and binding by Thomson-Shore, Inc., Dexter, Michigan

Library of Congress Cataloging-in-Publication Data

Greenberg, Martin, 1918 Feb. 3–
   The Hamlet vocation of Coleridge and Wordsworth.

   Includes index.
      1. English poetry—19th century—History and criti-
cism.   2. Romanticism—England.   3. Coleridge, Samuel
Taylor, 1772–1834—Criticism and interpretation.
4. Wordsworth, William, 1770–1850—Criticism and inter-
pretation.   5. Spirituality in literature.   6. Poets,
English—19th century—Biography.   I. Title.
PR571.G74   1986   821'.7'09   85-18189
ISBN 0-87745-131-1

FOR PAULA, AGAIN

CONTENTS

As long as man was himself nature—I mean pure nature, of course, not raw—he acted as an integrated sensuous being, a harmonious whole. Sense and reason, the receptive faculties and the faculties of action, had not yet parted company in him, much less come into contradiction. His feelings were not vague and inconsequent, without form, his thoughts an empty exercise of the imagination, without content; the former were governed by the law of necessity, the latter by reality. But when man arrived in the state of civilization and felt the hand of art laid on him, that harmony of the sensuous being was broken, and all that is possible to him now is moral unity, the aspiring to unity.

—Schiller, 1795

Every first movement, whatever is spontaneous, is beautiful, but every-thing is crooked, queer, as soon as it knows itself. Oh, the mind, the un-happy mind! Don't study too much, my dear boy.

—Kleist, 1806

Nothing is born by taking thought. That which is born comes of itself.

—D. H. Lawrence, 1916

Civilization is built upon a renunciation of instinct.

—Freud, 1930

Knowledge increases unreality.

—Yeats, 1939

Before Romanticism the intellectual did not exist, because there was no line of demarcation between life and learning. . . . To perceive that life is more important than thought, means being a learned man, an intellectual, it means that his own thought has not become life.

—Pavese, 1943

PREFACE

My subject is the Hamlet vocation of Coleridge and Wordsworth. By their Hamlet vocation I mean their being "called," each in his own way, to a life of inwardness, introspection, mind—with all its dangers. What dangers? The dangers of the reflective mind split apart from the effective will; spirituality parted from vitality, from human life and action; in Wordsworth's own language: knowledge and self-knowledge purchased by the loss of power. But this is an actual condition rather than a danger only threatening—the condition of the man of modern civilization, which Schiller describes as a rupture in the natural harmony of his sensuous being, Freud as a sacrifice of his natural instincts.

Wordsworth and Coleridge were so very different, as poets, as minds, as men. For this reason there has always been a tendency to side with one or the other. The nineteenth century sided with Wordsworth; our own time has swung over to Coleridge—a swing over of students and scholars rather than readers, both poets having meanwhile passed (along with poetry in general) from being life to being literature. An Italian lady I was recently introduced to surprised me very pleasantly by how well she knew the two (for they are such *English* poets and have never travelled well). A great admirer of Coleridge, she challenged me to say whose side I was on; she suspected it was Wordsworth's, because my answer didn't seem straightforward. (I was trying to say how much I had loved them both from youth.) But as different as the two men were, they were also drawn together into a friendship unique in the history of poetry. Though these two great poets did not have brilliant lives, their friendship was brilliant.

It's true that the friendship owed a great deal to Coleridge's being so forthcoming—so welcoming of, so encouraging to, so understanding of Wordsworth. Psychologically, perhaps, Coleridge made the friendship. But the friendship also had an essential metaphysical element, if I may express it so—mind. Here too Coleridge was the stimulus, by awakening Wordsworth to his own inwardness, by calling him to be, along with himself, an introspectionist, a "self-haunting spirit," as Wordsworth put it in *The Prelude*—by calling him, so positively, to a life of meditation and mind. But if Coleridge was the one who called, Wordsworth was very quick to answer.

Coleridge's Hamletism was well known to himself and his own age, better known to his than ours, because we are so impressed by his literary and philosophical intelligence, by his "myriad-mindedness," by the "seminality" of his thought. We think of him busy, and famous, as a seed scatterer. But he wanted to raise forests. His outcries against himself, which he made all his life, for always getting ready to do but never doing, are anguished. For Coleridge, the Hamlet vocation was a tragic one. It can be summed up succinctly: hypertrophy of the thinking man and atrophy of the natural man. By "abstruse research," as he exclaims in *Dejection*, he "stole from his own nature all the natural man." The death of the natural man meant Coleridge's death-in-life—a phrase, turned around as Life-in-Death, that appears as early as *The Ancient Mariner*. Involved in Coleridge's death as a natural man was his death as a poet; for his "shaping spirit of Imagination," he cries in the *Dejection*, was "what *nature* gave him at his birth"; imagination was an activity of the natural man. For Coleridge poetry was ultimately nature; and Wordsworth, as a poet, was a natural man as he himself was not, a *doing* man, a happy man.

Wordsworth agreed with Coleridge: he was a happy man. True enough, he was a passivist, but a wise passivist, which is to say an active passivist who by militant meditation healed the rupture between the modern mind and nature, reunited being. However, this only happened in moods ("that blessed mood"), moodily, in spots ("spots of time"), spottily. To provide the reunification of being with a stable foundation in a system of human understanding and feeling, was the great aim of Wordsworth's epic-philosophical project of "The Recluse," a project born out of the delighted talk of the two young friends in the heyday of their friendship. But Wordsworth was never able to write "The Recluse"; he was never even able to begin it. Instead he wrote a long poem, *The Prelude*, about writing a great poem. But for Wordsworth *The Prelude* did not make up for his failure with "The Recluse."

Like Hamlet, like Coleridge, Wordsworth in the end was defeated by self-division—but only in the end. The whole tendency of his imagination was toward severity, sublimity; it was to soar, Alp-like, above the common life of men and women into prophetic blank tremendousness. And just because of that tendency Wordsworth mistrusted his own imagination, though he also honored it. The great aim of his life was to unite sublime imagination with human tenderness, on the largest scale, and in that way give modern life something that it lacked and missed: a supreme epic work, meditative rather than martial, in which it might find and know itself. But he couldn't do it. The union of human tenderness and sublime imagination, which he was able to realize in short bursts of song, lyrically, proved impossible to him in epic song—in great story, great design. And not only to him.

Coleridge and Wordsworth, who were so very different, were different in their Hamletism. For Coleridge it was a desert of inanition, paralysis, a falling below the level of nature, out of human life, into impotent intellection. For Wordsworth, "aloft ascending, breathing in worlds / To which the

Heaven of Heavens is but a veil," the Hamlet vocation was to rise above the level of nature, above the common life, prepotently, into the infinite, which was also a desert. Yet each wished for the same thing, for what we all wish for: unity of being, to be whole.

In writing about Coleridge and Wordsworth, one's general debt to others is immense. But I should like to acknowledge my specific debt to Schiller's essay "On Naive and Sentimental Poetry" and A. C. Bradley's Oxford Lecture on Wordsworth. In spite of time they keep all their essential vitality. Among works by critics of our own day I owe a special debt to Geoffrey Hartman's book *Wordsworth's Poetry*, its brilliance undimmed after twenty years. And as I was working on this book, in the back of my mind an argument was always going on with Lionel Trilling, with his essays on Wordsworth and the "adversary culture." His influence, as always, has been a lively one for me—in this instance lively in opposition.

I should also like to express my gratitude to the Research Committee of C. W. Post College for awarding me a grant which made writing this book easier.

ONE

Samuel Taylor Coleridge

"A SMACK OF HAMLET"

A self-contemplating shadow
In enormous labours occupied.
                    —Blake

*T*oward the end of his life, after holding forth once again on his theory about Hamlet's character—that it consists in "the prevalence of the abstracting and generalizing habit over the practical," with the result that "every incident sets him thinking" and he continually neglects his duty of doing—Coleridge added the remark, "I have a smack of Hamlet myself, if I may say so."[1] He wasn't letting any cats out of the bag by this confession. Fifteen years before, in the winter of 1811–12, when he had lectured on Shakespeare with immethodical, intermittent, and sometimes borrowed brilliance, he wound up his account of *Hamlet*, according to Henry Crabb Robinson, by pointing out the moral of the play: "'Action,' he said, 'is the great end of all. No intellect, however grand, is valuable if it draw us from action and lead us to think and think till the time of action is passed by and we can do nothing.' Somebody said to me [Robinson continued], 'This is a satire on himself.'—'No,' said I, 'it is an elegy.'"[2] So in the very lecture hall in which Coleridge first expounded his idea of Hamlet's character, his own character was so much in the possession of his audience that they could smile knowingly at the resemblance between the two. Few English literary geniuses have been so ingenuous (and disingenuous!) as Coleridge.

From his earliest years he needed to unburden himself to others (and to himself), unpack his heart with words. In 1787 the schoolboy wrote from Christ's Hospital to a brother that he had "no one, to whom I can open my heart in full confidence. I wish you would remedy that evil by keeping up an epistolary correspondence with me." This was at the age of fourteen. Muteness was death for him; though it is a question whether his compulsion to put things into words, to articulate and explicate and expatiate—to realize the world to himself in utterance (which was at the same time to fend it off)—was not, like his Ancient Mariner's same speaking-compulsion, a species of life-in-death. A letter writer to the tune of six fat volumes, an inveterate notebook keeper and diarist of his mind, an annotator of margins and one of the champion talkers of all time, "he seems," in the words of Virginia Woolf, "not a man, but a swarm, a cloud, a buzz of words, darting this way and that, clustering, quivering, and hanging suspended." Coleridge's life was one long outpouring of language. And running through all the words, like a stream within a stream, was the subject of himself, the *problem* of himself, which never ceased to baffle him. Keats describes running into him on a Sunday-morning walk to Highgate in the spring of 1819:

> I walked with him at his alderman-after-dinner pace for nearly two miles I suppose. In those two Miles he broached a thousand things—let me see if I can give you a list—Nightingales, Poetry—on Poetical Sensation—Metaphysics—Different genera and species of Dreams—Nightmare—a dream accompanied by a sense of touch—single and double touch—A dream related— First and second consciousness—the difference explained between will and Volition—so many metaphysicians from a want of smoking the second consciousness—Monsters—the Kraken— Mermaids—Southey believes in them—Southey's belief too much diluted—A Ghost story—Good morning—I heard his voice as he came towards me—I heard it as he moved away—I had heard it all the interval—if it may be called so. He was civil enough to ask me to call on him at Highgate.

Keats is a young poet listening to an old talker, and his astonishment at such volubility is wry. But his list is a pretty fair Coleridge index; Keats was a good listener. And lurking in the list is the ever-present "Coleridge problem," in the phrase about "the difference explained between will and Volition." What this scholastical-sounding distinction meant to Coleridge, what it meant to him on his flesh and nerves, we can gather, among a lifetime of testimonies, from a letter of May 14, 1814, full of self-knowledge, self-accusation, self-pity and self-deception:

> By the long long Habit of the accursed Poison [opium] my Volition (by which I mean the faculty *instrumental* to the Will, and by which alone the Will can realize itself—it's [*sic*] Hands, Legs, & Feet, as it were) was completely deranged, at times frenzied, dissevered itself from the Will, & became an independent faculty: so that I was perpetually in the state, in which you may have seen paralytic Persons, who attempting to push a step forward in one direction are violently forced round to the opposite. I was sure that no ease, much less pleasure, would ensue: nay, was certain of an accumulation of pain. But tho' there was no prospect, no gleam of Light before, an indefinite indescribable Terror as with a scourge of ever restless, ever coiling and uncoiling Serpents, drove me on from behind.—The worst was, that in *exact proportion* to the *importance* and *urgency* of any Duty was it, as of a fatal necessity, sure to be neglected: because it added to the Terror above described. . . . What crime is there scarcely which has not been included in or followed from the one guilt of taking opium? Not to speak of ingratitude to my maker for the wasted Talents; of ingratitude to so many friends who have loved me I know not why; of barbarous neglect of my family. . . . I have in this one dirty business of Laudanum an hundred times deceived, tricked, nay, actually & consciously LIED.—And yet *all* these vices are so opposite to my nature, that but for this *free-agency-annihilating* Poison, I verily believe that I should have suffered myself to have been cut to pieces rather than have committed any one of them.[3]

His "will" is his intention and he intends only what is good. But his "volition," or the power of realizing his intentions, has been "dissevered" from his will by his enslavement to opium so that he is like a paralytic who in struggling to move forward finds himself jerked around and flung backwards by his own efforts. He is a moral cripple. This description of himself is vivid with the shame and anguish of impotence. Yet it is also self-exculpatory. Coleridge, as he often did, derives all his "vices" and "crimes" from "the one guilt" of his opium habit. But he knows that he stumbled into addiction inadvertently ("I was seduced into the ACCURSED Habit ignorantly"[4]); this was at a time when medical science still knew little about the drug and people were swallowing laudanum almost as they do aspirin today. So he is not really guilty of the one "crime" from which all the others followed, and therefore he is not guilty at all. Coleridge has let himself off the hook.

But writing at other times and to other correspondents, he knew better than this. He confessed to William Godwin in January 1802 that his inability to *do* (and *not* to do), his lack of "self-command," was as much a cause as an effect of his infirmities, especially that chief infirmity, his opium habit:

> The same causes, that have robbed me to so great a degree of the self-impelling self-directing Principle, have deprived me too of the due powers of Resistances to Impulses from without. If I might so say, I am, as an *acting* man, a creature of mere Impact. "I will" & "I will not" are phrases, both of them equally, of rare occurrence in my dictionary. . . . I evade the sentence of my own Conscience by no quibbles of self-adulation; I ask for Mercy indeed on the score of my ill-health; but I confess, that this very ill-health is as much an effect as a cause of this want of steadiness & self-command;* and it is for mercy that I ask, not for justice.[5]

And at the end of his life, in the *Epitaph* he wrote for himself, he was still asking for mercy for himself—though not instead of justice now, but instead of fame:

> Stop, Christian passer-by!—Stop, child of God,
> And read with gentle breast. Beneath this sod

---

*Earl Leslie Griggs emphasizes in his introduction to Volume 3 of the *Collected Letters* that "since as early as 1796 he [Coleridge] had resorted to laudanum to relieve mental agitation," as well as to relieve his physical pains.

A poet lies, or that which once seem'd he.
O, lift one thought in prayer for S.T.C.;
That he who many a year with toil of breath
Found death in life, may here find life in death!
Mercy for praise—to be forgiven for fame
He ask'd, and hoped, through Christ. Do thou the same!

Hazlitt, who was only a few years younger than Coleridge, remembered him from the days of their youth as "the only person I ever knew who answered to the idea of a man of genius." Where Keats only heard the owl in the elder poet's unpausing drawl, Hazlitt had heard in the soaring talk of the young poet and philosopher the high-flying bird of the imagination:

He talked on for ever; and you wished him to talk on for ever. His thoughts did not seem to come with labour and effort; but as if borne on the gusts of genius, and as if the wings of his imagination lifted him from off his feet. His voice rolled on the ear like the pealing organ, and its sound alone was the music of thought. His mind was clothed with wings; and raised on them he lifted philosophy to heaven.[6]

But Hazlitt learned to dislike Coleridge and despised him as a waster of his genius. Coleridge's "nose," he wrote, "the rudder of the face, the index of the will, was small, feeble, nothing—like what he has done."[7] He talked his life away: "la[id] down his pen to make sure of an auditor, and mortgage[d] the admiration of posterity for the stare of an idler. Mr. Coleridge . . . delights in nothing but episodes and digressions, neglects whatever he undertakes to perform, and can act only on spontaneous impulses, without object or method."[8]

At first, when Coleridge was still a very young man, he understood the stupor of his will, his "deranged volition," purely morally, as the vice of indolence. At the age of twenty-two he wrote to his brother George (November 6, 1794):

There is a vice of such powerful Venom, that one Grain of it will poison the overflowing Goblet of a thousand Virtues. This Vice

Constitution seems to have implanted in me, and Habit has
made it almost omnipotent. It is INDOLENCE! . . . Anxieties that
stimulate others, infuse an additional narcotic into my mind.
The appeal of Duty to my Judgement, and the pleadings of affection at my Heart—have been heard indeed—and heard with
deep regard—Ah! that they had been as constantly obeyed—But
so it has been—Like some poor Labourer whose Night's sleep
has but imperfectly refreshed his overwearied frame, I have sate
in drowsy uneasiness—and doing nothing have thought, what
a deal I had to do![9]

Later on this moral judgment on himself is sophisticated
into a psycho-philosophical analysis of his "continually divided Being." A notebook entry of 1805 reads:

All the realities about me lose their natural *healing* powers, at
least, diminish the same, & become not worthy of a Thought.
Who that thus lives with a continually divided Being can remain
healthy! [*At this point he inserted the following at a later time:* And
who can long remain body-crazed, & not at times use unworthy
means of making his Body the fit instrument of his mind? Pain
is easily subdued compared with continual uncomfortableness—
and the sense of stifled Power!—O this is that which made poor
Henderson, Collins, Boyce, &c &c &c—*Sots!*—awful Thought—
O it is horrid!—Die, my Soul, die!—Suicide—rather than this,
the worst state of Degradation! It is less a suicide! S.T.C.] I work
hard, I do the duties of common Life from morn to night / but
verily—I raise my limbs, "like lifeless *Tools*"—The organs of motion & outward action perform their functions at the stimulus of
a galvanic fluid applied by the *Will*, not by the Spirit of Life that
makes Soul and Body one.

These painful thoughts about the division in his being prompt
him to philosophize about unity of being: "Thought and Reality two distinct corresponding Sounds, of which no man can
say positively which is the Voice and which the Echo." And by
way of illustration of this perfect union of inward thought and

outward reality, he recalls the weeds in the fountain or natural well at Upper Stowey:

> The images of the weeds which hung down from its sides, appeared as plants growing up, straight and upright, among the water weeds that really grew from the Bottom / & so vivid was the Image, that for some moments & not till after I had disturbed the water, did I perceive that their roots were not neighbours, & they side-by-side companions. So—even then I said—so are the happy man's *Thoughts* and *Things*—(in the language of the modern Philosophers, Ideas and Impressions).[10]

But such a marriage of Thoughts and Things, of the mind which thinks and the world in which one acts, is reserved for happy men like Wordsworth and is denied to him.

Coleridge's analysis of Hamlet was part of his lifelong effort to grasp the problem of himself; he found his understanding of himself confirmed in Hamlet and his understanding of Hamlet confirmed in himself. But already in the twenty-two-year-old's letter to his brother George in 1794—"and doing nothing have thought, what a deal I have to do"—we hear the same accents, the same antithetical balancing of "doing nothing" against "resolving to do," that we find at the end of the thirty-nine-year-old's lecture on *Hamlet* in 1812:

> He is a man living in meditation, called upon to act by every motive human and divine, but the great object of his life is defeated by continually resolving to do, yet doing nothing but resolve.[11]

The November 6, 1794, letter had described Coleridge's indolence, figuratively, as a state of being drugged. This was prophetic. Six years or so later the figure of speech became a reality and Coleridge was a confirmed addict. This supports in its own way the truth of what he wrote to Godwin in 1802, that his opium illness was "as much an effect as a cause" of the illness of his soul. This 1794 letter is suggestive, too, about another of Coleridge's infirmities, his plagiarizing. In the letter he copied out some *Lines on a Friend Who Died of a Frenzy Fever Induced by Calumnious Reports* (the poem's title when published), which he had recently composed. Three days before, in copying the same verses into a letter to Robert Southey, he prefaced them with the remark that "a Friend of mine hath lately departed this Life in a frenzy fever induced by Anxiety! poor fellow—a child of frailty like me: yet he was amiable—!" [12] The man whom he thus singles out as a companion spirit in weakness (and amiability) was the Reverend Fulwood Smerdon; this clergyman had taken his father's place as vicar at Coleridge's Devonshire birthplace of Ottery St. Mary after the elder Coleridge's death in 1781. The poem elegizes one in whom "the finer Virtues" had been blighted by "wan Indolence." Looking into himself, Coleridge discovers just such a "sloth-jaundic'd" soul as his older friend's:

> With introverted Eye I contemplate
> Similitude of Soul—perhaps of Fate!
> To me hath Heaven with liberal hand assign'd
> Energic Reason & a shaping Mind,
> The daring ken of Truth, the patriot's part,
> And Pity's Sigh, that breathes the gentle heart—
> Sloth-jaundic'd all! and from my graspless hand
> Drop Friendship's precious Pearls, like hour-glass sand.
> I weep—yet stoop not! the faint Anguish flows.
> A dreamy Pang in Morning's fev'rish Doze.

The fever Smerdon died of, says the title of the poem, was "induced by calumnious reports"; the poem itself speaks about Smerdon's being slandered; but there is no hint in the poem as to what these calumnies and slanders were. However, a sentence in Coleridge's letter to his brother makes it clear that Smerdon was being accused of plagiarism: "Poor Smerdon! the reports concerning His literary plagiarism (as far as concerns *my* assistance) are *falsehoods*." [13] So Smerdon may indeed have been guilty of "literary plagiarism." What is false, writes Coleridge, are the reports that he himself had any hand in it.

(He seems to have had a hand in "metamorphosing" sermons for his brother George: "I have sent you," he wrote from Cambridge in 1792, "a sermon metamorphosed from an obscure publication by vamping, transposition, &c—if you like it, I can send you two more of the same kidney."[14]) Out of the discrepancy in candor between the letter and the poem arises that slightly bad smell which is so familiar to students of Coleridge.

Thus in the one letter of November 6, 1794, written when he was just turned twenty-two, we already hear sounded the three themes which compose so much of the "Coleridge problem": "deranged volition," opium and plagiarism—the first two openly confessed, the last dissimulated and denied to others and to himself. The fact that they appear together in a letter written in his earliest manhood suggests—what you would suspect anyhow—that they are different manifestations of some original, profound infirmity, a primitive impotence.

About the sources of this impotence in Coleridge's earliest years one can only speculate. In what he says about his father and mother it is perhaps possible to make out a domestic opposition which implanted itself in Coleridge as the structure of his own self-division—that psychological self-division which was the stimulus to his intensely felt metaphysical sense of the division, the rupture, of reality into the opposed realms of subject and object, Thoughts and Things (his plain-English version of the German-derived subject-object), I AM and IT IS.*[15] His descriptions of his father, the Reverend John Coleridge, are full of delighted affection and amusement: his father was "a perfect Parson Adams" in his learning, good-

---

*This fine Coleridgian antithesis, bottomed in the rock of the elementary grammar of modern self-consciousness, came from a confirmed antithesist who never tired of proclaiming "the *antithetical* balance-loving nature of man."—SC II, 5. Coleridge threw it out in a remark recorded by Crabb Robinson. The latter had just lent him a copy of Spinoza. "In the course of a few minutes, while standing in the room, Coleridge kissed Spinoza's face at the title-page, said his book was his gospel, and in less than a minute added that his philosophy was, after all, false. Spinoza's system had been demonstrated

heartedness, absentmindedness, and "excessive ignorance of the world," [16] who "used regularly to delight his village flock, on Sundays, with Hebrew quotations in his sermons, which he always introduced as the 'immediate language of the Holy Ghost.'" [17]

The elder Coleridge was indifferent to the good and evil of this world. As part of this indifference he did not trouble himself much about educating his sons to be gentlemen, except that he intended Samuel to follow him into the church.

My Father (who had so little of parental ambition in him, that he had destined his children to be Blacksmiths &c, & had accomplished his intention but for my Mother's pride & spirit of aggrandizing her family) my father had however resolved, that I should be a Parson. I read every book that came in my way without distinction—and my father was fond of me, & used to take me on his knees, and hold long conversations with me. I remember, that at eight years old I walked with him one winter evening from a farmer's house, a mile from Ottery—& he told me the names of the stars—and how Jupiter was a thousand times larger than our world—and that the other twinkling stars were Suns that had worlds rolling round them—& when I came home, he shewed me how they rolled round—/. I heard him with a profound delight & admiration: but without the least mixture of wonder or incredulity. For from my early reading of Faery Tales, & Genii &c &c—my mind had been habituated *to the Vast*—& I never regarded *my senses* in any way as the criteria of my belief. I regulated all my creeds by my conceptions not by my *sight*— even at that age. . . . —I have known some who have been *rationally* educated, as it is styled. They were marked by a microscopic acuteness; but when they looked at great things, all became a blank & they saw nothing—and denied (very il-

---

to be false, but only by that philosophy which has at the same time demonstrated the falsehood of all other philosophies. Did philosophy commence in an IT IS instead of an I AM, Spinoza would be altogether true; and without allowing breathing time he parenthetically asserted: 'I, however, believe in all the doctrines of Christianity, even of the Trinity.'"—*Henry Crabb Robinson on Books and Their Writers*, ed. Morley (1938), I, 112.

logically) that anything could be seen; and uniformly put the
negation of a power for the possession of a power—& called
the want of imagination Judgment, & the never being moved to
rapture Philosophy!— . . . He was an Israelite without guile;
simple, generous, and, taking some scripture texts in their literal
sense, he was conscientiously indifferent to the good & evil
of this world.[18]

About "my revered Father," Coleridge said, "I have a feeling,
one third pride & two thirds tenderness in being told that I
strongly resemble him in person & mind."[19] He speaks little
about his mother, and with little affection. De Quincey says
that "he was almost an object of persecution to his mother;
why, I could never learn." In the Coleridge family it was
the mother who whipped the children when they were bad,
pressed to have them educated, felt it was a humiliation for
her youngest son Samuel to go as a charity boy to the Christ's
Hospital school after her husband's death. (She wanted the
Charterhouse.) Coleridge's father had managed to rise into
the gentility by educating himself into a clergyman, but he
had exhausted all his ambition in doing so. It was the mother's
energy which drove the children on and made sure that they
would not fall back among the common people.

The spirit spoke through the vicar Coleridge to his son, the
world through the vicar's wife—parsonical abstractedness
and tenderheartedness as against hard-driving pride and fa-
milial aggrandizement; the stars of heaven as against bread
and cheese; the vasty deep of the "one & indivisible" revealed
to the imaginative mind as against the "little things" of the
senses.* Much the same opposition was present in Coleridge's own marriage. That shadowy figure the Reverend Fulwood Smerdon, that "child of frailty" like himself, who took
his father's place as the Ottery vicar, is again a suggestive

---

* "I can *at times* feel strongly the beauties, you describe . . . but more frequently *all things* appear little . . . the universe itself—what but an immense
heap of *little* things?—!—My mind feels as if it ached to behold & know
something *great*—something *one & indivisible.* . . ."—CL I, 349.

presence here. At the age of nineteen Coleridge had written some lively flippant lines about the vicar Smerdon and his wife to his brother George:

> Tho' much averse at folk to flicker,
> To find the Simile for Vicar
> I've made thro' Earth, and Air, and Sea
> A Voyage of Discovery—
> And let me add (to ward off strife)
> For Vicar & for Vicar's Wife.
> She gross & round beyond belief,
> A Superfluity of Beef:
> Her mind and body of a piece
> And both compos'd of Kitchen Grease—
> In short, Dame Truth might safely dub her
> "Vulgarity enclos'd in Blubber."
> He, meagre Bit of Littleness,
> All Snuff, and Musk, and Politesse,
> So thin, that strip him of his clothing
> He'd totter on the Edge of Nothing—
> In case of Foe he well might hide
> Snug in the Collops of *her* side.
> Ah then—what simile can suit?
> Spindle Leg in great Jack Boot?
> Pismire crawling in a Rutt?
> Or a Spiggot in a Butt?
> So I Ha'd and Hem'd awhile,
> When Mrs. Memory with a smile
> Thus twitch'd my Ear—"Why sure, I ween
> In London Streets thou oft has seen
> The very image of this Pair.
> A Little Ape with large she bear
> Tied by hapless chain together,
> An unlick'd mass the One—the other
> An Antic lean with nimble crupper—"
> But stop, my Muse! for here comes Supper.[20]

The poem is making fun of a little, mincing man and his fat wife. But doesn't it also signal a recognition of the "Similitude of Soul—perhaps of Fate!" that Coleridge saw between himself and Smerdon two years later? "Littleness" and "Politesse" are antagonistically yoked together with a "Superfluity of Beef"; spirit so fastidious and unfleshed as to threaten to dwindle into nothingness, with "Vulgarity enclos'd in Blubber"; ignominious puniness ("Spindle Leg") with coarse strength ("great Jack Boot")—yet the "Antic lean" is "nimble" and the "she bear" is an "unlick'd mass." What the poem suggests, if you read it for intimations of the poet himself, is Coleridge's sense of his littleness, verging on nullity, as a spiritual man, his sense of being smothered in the grossness of a Brobdingnagian practical world of flesh and kitchen grease, and in the grossness too of his own obstructed self; against which world his spiritual strivings are so many infant-Gulliver squirmings in the fist of mast-high grown-ups—yet it is a world he can divert by his mental nimbleness, as Coleridge was to divert the world by his conversations and his lectures.

He himself commented *"a good Line"* about Smerdon "tottering on the Edge of Nothing" when he copied the poem out in a letter to his brother George. That tottering on the edge of nothing became in later life Coleridge's permanent state; he called it death-in-life and gladly rendered it up, in his epitaph, in the hope of life-in-death with Christ, after a lifetime of mental fight against it as a poet and a philosopher. His assertion of the living power of the spirit—of idea, imagination, reason—against the dead weight of spiritless mechanism "was no abstract matter with him," as I. A. Richards writes, "but a daily torment. . . . [H]e had to extricate himself from the Locke tradition, not because it was 'false,' but because for himself, at some hours, it was too painfully true. It was the intellectual equivalent of his uncreative moods, and of the temper of an uncreative century." [21] These "moods" were more than moods; they were a primitive, ultimate sense of his own spirit as puny, ineffectual, "unmanly," * lapsing into unreal-

---

* A word he often applied to himself.

ity—a pismire crawling in the great rut of the world. Such was his particular situation. But such, too, was the situation spirituality in general was arriving at toward the end of the eighteenth century as the might of scientific materialism, collecting itself into machines, began to transform with hammer blows the practical life of England and the world.

In 1931 E. M. Forster wrote that "posterity . . . has never ceased to hold up her plump finger to Coleridge, and shake it and say that he has disappointed her."[22] But that was the older posterity. The new posterity of today now shakes her finger at the old posterity for having been so moralistic, so self-complacent, so Victorian. And well she might. Carlyle's portrait of Coleridge in *The Life of John Sterling*, which added the colors of contempt to lineaments already sketched by Coleridge himself and his own generation, fixed the nineteenth century's picture of him: "The whole figure and air, good and amiable otherwise, might be called flabby and irresolute; expressive of weakness under the possibility of strength." Carlyle describes Coleridge as wandering unintelligibly in a "Kantean haze-world." "I still recollect his 'object' and 'subject,' terms of continual recurrence in the Kantean province; and how he sang and snuffled them into 'om-m-mject' and 'sum-m-mject,' with a kind of solemn shake or quaver, as he rolled along." And Carlyle winds up on a note of brutal sanctimoniousness:

> The truth is, I now see, Coleridge's talk and speculation was the emblem of himself: in it as in him, a ray of heavenly inspiration struggled, in a tragically ineffectual degree, with the weakness of flesh and blood. He says once, he 'had skirted the howling deserts of Infidelity'; this was evident enough: but he had not had the courage, in defiance of pain and terror, to press resolutely across said deserts to the new firm lands of Faith beyond. . . . For pain, danger, difficulty, steady slaving toil, and other highly disagreeable behests of destiny, shall in no wise be shirked by

any brightest mortal that will approve himself loyal to his mission in the world.[22a]

To the nineteenth century Coleridge was "tragically ineffectual," his actual accomplishments, like his nose (as Hazlitt said), "small, feeble, nothing." To us today, however, his nothings—his "episodes and digressions" and fragments—are worth more than a library of finished works by others. Think only of *Kubla Khan* (and never mind his notebooks, essays, letters, lecture notes, and unpublished manuscripts). If that "fragment," as Coleridge called it in his subtitle, were to fall out of English poetry, what a hole it would leave! Yet Coleridge was more on Hazlitt's side than ours. To him the poem was a fragment—one more item in the long list of his incompletions. He had started what looked like a romantic narrative poem about Kubla Khan and his paradisal gardens and then broke off after two stanzas, unable to go on, adding only a yearning last stanza, a kind of postscript (perhaps at a later time), about his not being able to go on.[23] Yet the postscript is a cry of triumph as well as yearning about how the poet

>   would build that dome in air,
>   That sunny dome! those caves of ice!

if only he were able to recreate the song of the Abyssinian maid:

>   And all who heard should see them there,
>   And all should cry, Beware! Beware!
>   His flashing eyes, his floating hair!
>   Weave a circle round him thrice,
>   And close your eyes with holy dread,
>   For he on honey-dew hath fed,
>   And drunk the milk of Paradise.

How is it that the note of triumphant peroration doesn't sound anomalous in an aborted composition? Something happens to the poem which rescues it from defeat, from being *just* a fragment. One way perhaps to describe what happens is the indirect one of trying to describe what happens to the poet: Coleridge's fundamental life-feeling, of great power straining against powerlessness ("the sense of stifled Power!"), overturns from below the narrative poem he meant to write. He set out to tell a story of some scope in verse, something pointing in the epic direction, though only pointing that way; for to really write an epic poem, he said,

> I should not think of devoting less than 20 years. . . . Ten to collect materials and warm my mind with universal science. I would be a tolerable Mathematician, I would thoroughly know Mechanics, Hydrostatics, Optics, and Astronomy, Botany, Metallurgy, Fossilism, Chemistry, Geology, Anatomy, Medicine—then the *mind of man*—then the *minds of men*—in all Travels, Voyages and Histories. So I would spend ten years—the next five to the composition of the poem—and the five last to the correction of it.[24]

His intention in *Kubla Khan* is to write something more ambitious than a lyrical poem; but his ambition, always tending to megalomania under the incitement of his impotence, swells up into a self-defeating monster. Even the suggestion of epicality leads on for him into something requiring such extraordinary, such heroic exertions on his part as to shipwreck on itself. *Kubla Khan* the narrative poem sinks before it starts in the too-much of Coleridge's delirious conception of poetic magnitude.

But meanwhile the true voice of feeling in the poet, not to be denied, seizes hold, from the very first line, of the ambitious poem the poet can't write and wrests it over into a poem *about* the poem he can't write, a despairing-triumphant poem about the poet's efforts to *be* a poet, to be one of "the true Protoplasts, Gods of Love who tame the Chaos."[25] Wordsworth's *Prelude* too is about the poet's effort to be a poet and to prepare himself to write the great poem which he never wrote; it too fails to achieve real unity and remains a kind of fragment, though on the largest scale. The great modern lit-

erature is full of—*consists* of, I am tempted to say—great fragments. Writing poetry, for Coleridge, was more than a personal problem. It raised for him the problem of what a poet is,
which, as he writes in the *Biographia Literaria*, "is so nearly the
same question" with what poetry is "that the answer to the
one is involved in the solution of the other." [26] Coleridge's personal problem of being a poet merged with the problematicalness, in the modern world, of poetry itself. In *Kubla Khan*
poetry itself becomes the never-to-be-fully-attained object of
romantic yearning.

In his preface Coleridge remarked, with false offhanded-
ness, that he was publishing the poem almost twenty years
after its composition "rather as a psychological curiosity, than
on the ground of any supposed *poetic* merits." Not only was it
just a fragment, it was just a psychological curiosity! *Kubla
Khan* entered the world with almost crawling apologetical-
ness. More than a century and a half later you want to give its
author a shake for having been so abject. You want to give him
a double shake for boasting at the same time, under cover of
treating the poem as a freak, about his being such an inspired
poet, a vessel of the divine wind. For the psychological interest he claims for the poem in his preface is that of its having
been composed "in a profound sleep" which followed his taking a dose of opium—"if," he says, "that indeed can be called
composition in which all the images rose up before him as
things, with a parallel production of the correspondent expressions, without any sensation or consciousness of effort."
Coleridge is saying: "I know you will think the poem is contemptible; I shan't defend it. Yet it proves its maker is one of
the truly inspired, one of those who—as Plato says in the
Ion—'like Bacchic maidens draw milk and honey from the
rivers when they are under the influence of Dionysus but not
when they are in their right mind.' So perhaps you shouldn't
think the poem contemptible after all."

Now Coleridge exaggerated to the point of falsification the
involuntary character of *Kubla Khan*'s composition. You don't

write great poems in your dreams; who knew that better than the Coleridge who required "judgement ever awake and steady self-possession" from the poet? A manuscript turned up in 1934 says, much more credibly, that the poem came to him "in a sort of Reverie"—but the reverie is a state of consciousness however relaxed, not of sleep, and is familiar enough ground for the poet who, unexempted from Adam's curse, has to labor at his craft in the sweat of his brow.* How Coleridge tries, by his disingenuous, boastful apologetical-ness, to drown an extraordinary work in confusion!

Nevertheless, his lack of confidence in himself and in *Kubla Khan* does not add up to just a case of his being poor-spirited, an unconfident genius. Behind his poor-spiritedness, mixed up with it, is something general, not special to him. What is working in him, in an early state of evolution, is the self-deprecation, the "shame" of the modern poet at not being able to be "truly great," to tell a great, a world-embracing *story*—to "tame the Chaos" like a Homer or a Shakespeare or a Milton by composing its jarring dissonant atoms into a history with a beginning, middle and end. Looking back at his great forebears, the modern poet is ashamed of his own impotence.

Today Coleridge has been justified and redeemed against himself and his own century. Yet we only misunderstand things in our own way when we turn the nineteenth-century Coleridge—the notorious procrastinator, opium addict, runner-off at the mouth, plagiarist, liar ("moral imbecile," his

*Wordsworth, when he was sixty years old, "told some undergraduates at Trinity College, Cambridge, that some of his best thoughts came to him 'between sleeping and waking, or as he expressed it, in a morning sleep.' The observation was recorded in his diary by Henry Alford, one of the undergraduates, and arose out of a discussion of 'Kubla Khan,' which Wordsworth thought Coleridge might have composed in the same half-awake state in which some of his own poems came to him. Wordsworth certainly attached a special importance to 'the first, involuntary thoughts upon waking in the morning.' He once told R. P. Graves, the Vicar of Ambleside, that they ought to be watched closely 'as indications of the real current of moral being.'"— F. W. Bateson, *Wordsworth: A Re-Interpretation* (1954), 192.

brother-in-law Southey unkindly called him[27])—upside down
and treat him in a spirit of triumphant vindication. Coleridge
did fail, though not in *Kubla Khan*—there he misunderstood
himself and what he had done. Coleridge *was* a plagiarist—
there he *wished* to misunderstand himself and deceive others.
We insult his life, the mystery of his life, and his lifelong anguish when we smother his agonized outcries about failed
efforts and wasted talents in the bosom of our sympathy. Justice has been done him, but at the cost of blurring the Coleridge that Coleridge himself describes, the Coleridge who
was helpless in the grip of his impotence and inanition:

> All nature seems at work. Slugs leave their lair—
> The bees are stirring—birds are on the wing—
> And Winter slumbering in the open air,
> Wears on his smiling face a dream of Spring!
> And I the while, the sole unbusy thing,
> Nor honey make, nor pair, nor build, nor sing.
>
> *(Work Without Hope)*

In later life Coleridge sometimes tried to argue that his record was after all not just a blank. He defended himself in the
Biographia Literaria against the "rumor of having dreamed
away [his] life to no purpose," by citing various accomplishments (*not* including his poetry). But his exculpation of himself lacks confidence—and dignity—and turns into the familiar inculpation, which is uttered with touching dignity: "By
what I *have* effected, am I to be judged by my fellow men;
what I *could* have done, is a question for my own conscience.
On my own account I may perhaps have had sufficient reason
to lament my deficiency in self-control, and the neglect of
concentering my powers to the realization of some permanent
work. But to verse rather than to prose, if to either, belongs
the 'voice of mourning' for

> . . . .
> Sense of past youth, and manhood come in vain,
> And genius given and knowledge won in vain;

And all which I had culled in wood-walks wild,
And all which patient toil had rear'd, and all
Commune with thee had open'd out—but flowers
Strew'd on my corpse, and borne upon my bier
In the same coffin, for the self-same grave!"[28]

Coleridge is quoting from his own poem *To William Wordsworth*, written right after hearing the latter read the completed *Prelude* aloud to him—to Wordsworth genius had not been given in vain.

To take Coleridge seriously is to take seriously his feelings of defeat, to take seriously his *actual* defeat. (There the "moralistic" nineteenth century understood him better.) It is to take his plagiarisms seriously, rather than ignoring or minimizing them or explaining them away with elaborate arguments. In his work *Coleridge and the Pantheist Tradition*, Professor McFarland is able to transcendentalize Coleridge's plagiarisms into a "mode of composition by mosaic organization": "For the very multiplicity of instances—far more than at first charged, and by no means as yet all identified—suggests the explanation, bizarre though it may seem, that we are faced not with plagiarism, but with nothing less than a mode of composition—composition by mosaic organization rather than by painting on an empty canvas."[29] Morally considered, this is the sheerest casuistry. Coleridge took from others without acknowledgement, vehemently denying it whenever he was caught out. That is called plagiarism. (He himself was quick enough—unpleasantly quick—to accuse others of it.) Never was there a plagiarist, it is true, with so much genius. But he *was* a plagiarist. Henry James catches this complexity when he says about the character he modelled after Coleridge in his story "The Coxon Fund," that "no man who was so much of an absorbent can ever have been so little of a parasite." But Coleridge *was* a parasite.*

---

*Coleridge's "parasitism" was as evident in his personal life as in his literary life. From 1808 to his death in 1834 he lived with—and in varying degrees

Coleridge's own way of enunciating this truth about himself is in the form of a finely stated general truth, the personal reference hidden in the abstraction: "To admire on principle, is the only way to imitate without loss of originality."[30] This is so; and it is often—though by no means always—so about his own "imitations." He was not a notable intellectual originator, but he was an original-minded interpreter of German profundities to the Anglo-Saxons,* an ebullient intellect, vivid sensibility, and (briefly) an extraordinary, supreme poet. René Wellek, after an introductory review of Coleridge's dependence on the German Romantics in his *History of Modern Criticism*, hastens to add that Coleridge was not "a mere echo of the Germans with no originality and no independence. . . . Rather, Coleridge combines the ideas he derived from Germany in a personal way, and he combines them moreover with elements of the eighteenth-century tradition of neoclassicism and British empiricism." He admired and imitated on principle, without losing his distinctive qualities of thought and feeling. But Coleridge used this complex truth to hide the simple lie of plagiarism; and the lie lay like a lump inside him, a part of that being blocked and stopped—of that "sense of stifled Power!"—which was his lifelong experience.

In a notebook entry belonging to the end of 1804, Coleridge tried to come to some kind of understanding with himself about what he called his "obligations":

> In the Preface of my Metaphys. Works I should say—Once & all read Tetens, Kant, Fichte, &c—& there you will trace or if you are on the hunt, track me. Why then not acknowledge your obligations step by step? Because, I could not do in a multitude

---

on—the Wordsworths at Allan Bank in Grasmere, the Morgans in London, and the Gillmans in Highgate, to name only his principal dependencies.

*John Stuart Mill said in his essay on Coleridge that "although Coleridge is to Englishmen the type and the main source" of German philosophical thought, "he is the creator rather of the shape in which it has appeared among us, than of the doctrine itself."—*On Bentham and Coleridge* (Harper Torchbooks, 1950), 103.

of glaring resemblances without a lie/ for they had been mine,
formed, & full formed in my own mind, before I had ever heard
of these Writers, because to have fixed on the partic. instances in
which I have really been indebted to these Writers would have
[been] very hard, if possible, to me who read for truth & self-
satisfaction, not to make a book, & who always rejoiced & was
jubilant when I found my own ideas well expressed already
by others, (& would have looked like a *trick*, to skulk there not
quoted,) & lastly, let me say, because (I am proud perhaps but) I
seem to know, that much of the matter remains my own, and that
the Soul is *mine*. I fear not him for a Critic who can confound a
Fellow-thinker with a Compiler.[31]

One is almost shocked by the ingenuousness with which he
speaks right off about being "hunted" and "tracked" down.
The image confesses openly what he then proceeds to deny,
in words which then shock by their disingenuousness. His argument is transparent, although his words are not: There is "a
multitude of glaring resemblances" between his ideas and
work already published by Tetens, Kant, Fichte, and others.
But to acknowledge these "resemblances" ("obligations") in-
dividually would be a "lie," because the ideas as ideas, apart
from the actual matter or words—the "Soul" of them—had
been his long before he had ever read these writers. He cannot put quotation marks about the sentences, paragraphs and
pages he took from others because that would make it appear
that the ideas were not his own. He lies, because not to lie
would be the greater lie.*

I think Professor McFarland has a point when he calls

---

*When it came to laying claim to the "soul" of ideas, works, and discoveries
Coleridge could become quite mad: He had conceived the idea of *Childe
Harold* and sketched its plan long before Byron wrote his poem; he had discovered Goethe's theory of colors before Goethe (and would have published it
but for Southey's diverting his attention to poetry); he had had the idea of a
better, more original *Faust* before he had ever seen Goethe's *Faust*; he had an-
ticipated work by Faraday in acoustics; and so on and so on.—See Fruman,
83–85.

Coleridge's magpie way of grabbing up bits and pieces of others' work and fitting them together, an unusual "mode of composition" which arrived at something more than a bunch of extracts. Here he is following Coleridge in the latter's claim to be a "Fellow-thinker" of the German philosophers, not just a compiler of their thoughts. But Coleridge lied about what he did. And plagiarism is lying, not lack of originality—the moral defeat can't be cancelled. What depths of humiliation, skinned over by his denials to others and himself, there must have been for him in having to take and take without acknowledgement. Lurking in his Hamlet theory is a theory about modern life-defeat, and it came straight out of his own defeated life.

Crabb Robinson was right in calling Coleridge's *Hamlet* lecture an elegy on himself, not a satire. There was little of the satirical in Coleridge, not to speak of the self-satirical. As subtle and complex as his mind was, morally he was pledged to innocence, an often gushing innocence which shrank from irony, sardonicism, acerbity. He had no smack of that side of Hamlet! For Coleridge *Hamlet* was the tragedy of a man defeated by self-division. In reading the play in this way he elegized his own defeat by self-division. The last thing Coleridge was, or wished to be, was an impersonal reasoner. Feeling, a vehement personal accent—an ardent implication of himself in all that his mind entertains—runs through all his discursive writing, however abstract. One of the great introspectionists of modern times, he must have noticed this characteristic in himself at an early age; he was already mentioning it in a letter when he was twenty-four: "I feel strongly, and I think strongly; but I seldom feel without thinking, or think without feeling. . . . My philosophical opinions are blended with, or deduced from, my feelings: & this, I think, peculiarizes my style of Writing. And like everything else, it is sometimes a beauty, and sometimes a fault."[32]

As far as Coleridge's criticism of *Hamlet* is concerned, this mixing himself and his own feelings into, mixing himself up with Shakespeare's tragedy has been thought a fault rather than a beauty by twentieth-century criticism. At the start of the century, A. C. Bradley was already criticizing Coleridge's Hamlet for being too much like Coleridge himself, "on one side a man of genius, on the other side, the side of will, deplorably weak, always procrastinating and avoiding unpleasant duties, and often reproaching himself in vain"; whereas Shakespeare's Hamlet is a "quick and impetuous" man of action as well as a moody, self-involved monologuist—the slayer of Polonius, tripper-up of Rosencrantz and Guildenstern and finally the executioner of King Claudius himself.* And Bradley makes a joke: "Imagine Coleridge doing any of these things!" Well, I can't imagine it. But Bradley was insensitive to the philosophical suggestiveness of Coleridge's psychological description of Hamlet. He seems to have had little feeling for the problematic character of modern intellectuality and the modern pathos of self-consciousness. The idea that there might be something ambiguous or defeating about the vocation of thought, or, as he puts it, that "speculative thinking" might lead to irresolution in the affairs of life, he thinks an unexamined assumption. The most he will allow is that professors may be absentminded—that "absorption in *any* intellectual interest, together with withdrawal from affairs, may make a man slow and unskillful in affairs"; but "the notion that speculative thinking specially tends to produce" Hamlet's kind of irresolution "is really a mere illusion." And he winds

---

*Freud (among many others) made the same criticism of the view of Hamlet as an inactive type, as constitutionally incapable of acting: "Hamlet is far from being represented as a person incapable of taking any action. We see him doing so on two occasions; first in a sudden outburst of temper when he runs his sword through the eavesdropper behind the arras, and secondly in a premeditated and even crafty fashion, when, with all the callousness of a Renaissance prince, he sends the two courtiers to the death that had been planned for himself."—*Interpretation of Dreams* (Avon), 298.

up his argument against Coleridge* with that kind of inane checker-playing to which an unphilosophical literary psychologism is so prone: if Hamlet had heard from the Ghost inside of a week, before his mother's marriage to his uncle, he would have killed Claudius with all the determination of an Othello, "though probably after a longer and more anxious deliberation."

But the most powerful voice raised against the Coleridge Hamlet was T. S. Eliot's. Eliot did not really attack romantic "subjectivity"—the word is noticeably absent from "Tradition and the Individual Talent." What he attacked was the *autobiographical* emphasis of romantic subjectivity, its talking so openly about itself. (He himself was secretive.) What he called for was a poetry in which the poet's experience was transmuted by the catalytic action of his art into something new, impersonal, objectified, something raised above the pomp of personality in the poet, beyond the reach of biographical inquisitiveness in the critic, into a sphere of aesthetic inviolability—a dramatizing rather than a confessional poetry. It was still a poetry of the self, but a self whose tracks have been completely covered. Eliot attacked Coleridge's *Hamlet* criticism for being captious and slanted (as indeed it sometimes is); it was not "an honest inquiry as far as the data permit," he nastily remarked in 1923 in "The Function of Criticism," but "an attempt to present Coleridge in an attractive costume." However, the note of contempt, the suggestion of dishonesty, warn us that another Eliot, the doctrinaire, reactionary one, has taken over from Eliot the literary critic. This other Eliot was mounted on a neoclassical (Anglo-Catholic, Royalist) high horse and despising Coleridge (and Goethe) as shady ro-

---

*And against Schlegel. Bradley lumps the two men's views together into a common interpretation of *Hamlet* as a "tragedy of reflection." This is understandable; the two are branches from a common romantic trunk. Yet it is just here, in his Hamlet idea, that Coleridge owes *nothing* to Schlegel, though he owes him so much elsewhere in his Shakespeare criticism.

mantic types, flawed creative minds who vicariously worked out on Shakespeare. The doctrinaire Eliot who aggressively entered the lists as the champion of old orthodoxy against the modern decline and fall, did not care, indeed took satisfaction in the fact, that his high horse looked like a Rosinante to the age of H. G. Wells, Bertrand Russell, Sigmund Freud and John Middleton Murry. (The collocation of names is his.) Yet it was a Rosinante.* Like a Voltaire reborn, he calls *Hamlet* "an artistic failure" in his early essay "Hamlet and His Problems." To be sure, the play is more "interesting" (he puts the word between disdainful quotation marks) than an "assured artistic success" like *Coriolanus*; "but probably more people have thought *Hamlet* a work of art because they found it interesting, than have found it interesting because it is a work of art. It is the 'Mona Lisa' of literature."†

Eliot's eye, we notice, is more on the modern *Hamlet* audience, whom he wants to insult, than on the play itself. When he gets around to the play, when he gets *into* the play, there is a perceptible change: he leaves off sneering and becomes what he is when he is not being the scourge of modern heresies, a very great literary critic. The fault he finds with the tragedy is its failure to "objectify" Hamlet's feeling of intense disgust. We see nothing in the external circumstances of the play, he writes, which might account for—which might prop-

*Two decades later Eliot said so himself:
   We cannot revive old factions
   We cannot restore old policies
   Or follow an antique drum.

(*Little Gidding*)

†This passage never fails to make me smile: in compelled admiration for its snobbish hauteur, in deprecation of its perverse judgment. Of course there is an ignorant appreciation of great and famous works of art. But to suggest that the only thing *properly* interesting in a work of art is its art, is narrowly aesthetic in a way Eliot himself never really was. All his life he thought hard about the connection between art and belief. I suppose the young Eliot was irritated by Hamlet the celebrity, an early product of modern art publicity. That kind of publicity can turn you against anything.

erly *evoke*—such disgust, which is "in *excess* of the facts." The
visible life and action of the play—the "objective correlative"—is inadequate to express Hamlet's internal emotion,
whereas artistic success lies just precisely in the "complete
adequacy of the external to the emotion." Shakespeare was
unable to turn *Hamlet* into a tragedy that was "intelligible,
self-complete, in the sunlight." There is some stuff in it he
could not "drag to light" and which "therefore remain[ed] to
poison life and obstruct action."

> The levity of Hamlet . . . is the buffoonery of an emotion which
> can find no outlet in action; in the dramatist it is the buffoonery
> of an emotion which he cannot express in art. The intense feel-
> ing, ecstatic or terrible, without an object or exceeding its object,
> is something which every person of sensibility has known; it is
> doubtless a subject of study for pathologists. It often occurs in
> adolescence: the ordinary person puts these feelings to sleep, or
> trims down his feeling to fit the business world; the artist keeps
> it alive by his ability to intensify the world to his emotions. . . .
> [U]nder compulsion of what experience [Shakespeare] attempted
> to express the inexpressibly horrible, we cannot ever know.

This is brilliant criticism. But I find the eloquence of Eliot's
description of Hamlet surprising. It does not seem to jibe
with his adverse view of the play. Don't we have here a picture, painted in vivid, sympathetic colors, of the archetypally
romantic Hamlet—only framed in a negative neo-classicizing
judgment? There is something of Goethe's Hamlet in it—the
sensitive person who is unsuited to the business world and to
the business of the play; of the Coleridgian Hamlet drowning
in the "morbid excess" of his own interior consciousness, "for
ever occupied with the world within him, and abstracted
from external things";[33] of the nauseated Nietzschean Hamlet; of the Freudian Hamlet in the grip of an emotion neither
he nor his creator understands, paralyzed by something inside him he can't drag to light. And there is in it too the Titan
soul of the romantic Shakespeare, striving to express the in-

expressible. In his essay "On Poesy or Art," Coleridge had warned against the neo-classicizing "effort to combine together two incongruous things, that is to say, modern feelings in antique forms."[34] Eliot's essay is just such an incongruous effort to contain *Hamlet*'s modern problematicalness of feeling, to which he responds with palpable emotion, in an "antique" (Aristotelian) judgment. The dogmatic neo-classicizer and sneerer at psychology repudiates the mystery of feeling in *Hamlet* ("it is doubtless a subject of study for pathologists") even as he feels its force, by dismissing the play as an artistic failure.

How does Coleridge describe the mystery of feeling? In the same way Eliot does, as an inexplicable intensity, as something in excess of the facts: "Every human feeling is greater and larger than the exciting cause,—a proof, I think that man is designed for a higher state of existence; and this is deeply implied in music, in which there is always something more and beyond the immediate expression."[35] But for Coleridge *every* human feeling is in excess of the facts; emotion is *essentially* mysterious.* For the ultimate explanation of the mystery he looked prayerfully to the next world; emotions finally find their objective correlative in "a higher state of existence." He looked higher rather than lower, to God rather than into the depths. But this was not because he shut his eyes to the

---

*For Wordsworth, too. In *The Convention of Cintra* he writes: "the passions of men (I mean, the soul of sensibility in the heart of man)—in all quarrels, in all contests, in all quests, in all delights, in all employments which are either sought by men or thrust upon them—do immeasurably transcend their objects. The true sorrow of humanity consists in this;—not that the mind of man fails; but that the course and demands of action and of life so rarely correspond with the dignity and intensity of human desires. . . ."—PrW I, 339. In the Preface to the *Lyrical Ballads* he had already said about the poems that "the feeling therein developed gives importance to the action and situation, and not the action and situation to the feeling." Coleridge and Wordsworth thus turn Aristotle upside down. In the world of classical tragedy "the course and demands of action and of life" *do* correspond with the dignity and intensity of human desires"; in the romantic world man longs for "a higher state of existence."

depths. Over and over again, as his notebooks show, his "self-watching, subtilizing mind"* spied out the signs of unconscious mentality in himself. It was not only a matter of paying attention to his dreams. He felt the silent presence of the unconscious everywhere: in the little prosaic workings of the mind and at the farthest imaginative reaches, in questions of motive and conscience, at the heart of the struggle for self-knowledge; in his speculative castings about he is always liable to stumble on its traces. Writing about Wordsworth's *Immortality Ode* he remarks that it is only comprehensible to those who "had been accustomed to watch the flux and reflux of their inmost nature, to venture at times into the twilight realms of consciousness, and to feel a deep interest in modes of inmost being."[36] When Coleridge contemplated the unconscious in its benign (not its malign) workings, he called it the part of the man of genius which *is* his genius, the part of the mind-bottle below the narrow neck. The life and feeling were from there, impulse and imagination, the milk and honey-dew—all the natural man.

A self-doubting, self-scrutinizing, self-conscious genius, how Coleridge delighted in the wind of inspiration blowing from the nether regions and sweeping all before it, "when lulled Reason sleeps on the stormy Bosom of Transport, as a ship boy in the Shrouds."[37] (And how he lied about dashing things off in inspired fits when he had labored them out over weeks and months.[38]) Even when his unconscious mind became a source of terror to him he loved the rapture of abandonment to what comes unbidden—though now rather the *idea* of it, his actual experiences being too painful. Even for the later Coleridge, who "stresses the power of the 'conscious will' at the expense of Fancy and the law of association," as Patricia Adair writes,[39] the creative act remained a form of transport—the self transported out of itself, set free from itself, careless and superb. In a scintillating phrase in the

*This phrase occurs in an early version of *Frost at Midnight*.

Biographia Literaria, he speaks of the "madness prepense of Pseudo-poesy"*—true poetry is "mad" indeed, false poetry mad in craft, mad "prepensively." (Eliot's version of this, in "Tradition and the Individual Talent," is that "the bad poet is usually unconscious where he ought to be conscious, and conscious where he ought to be unconscious.")

Yet the unconscious, *his* unconscious, was a stone wall to his understanding; it stopped him dead. Coleridge was a sharp-eyed observer of consciousness in its various subtle gradations, not an analyst of unconsciousness, which defeated him. So he gave its understanding over to God:

> Without Drawing I feel myself but half invested with Language— Music too is wanting to me.—But yet tho' one should unite Poetry, Draftsman's-ship & Music—the greater & perhaps nobler certainly all the subtler parts of one's nature, must be solitary— Man exists herein to himself & to God alone / —Yea, in how much only to God—how much lies *below* his own consciousness.[40]

He gave it over to God all the more as the years advanced and nightmare confusion usurped the rule there, defeating his shaping spirit of imagination. "As he tried to finish [*Christabel*] through the years of opium haunted nightmares," Mrs. Adair writes, "Coleridge became bitterly aware of the presence of sin in the unconscious mind. . . . [T]he notebook entries of the time confirm an increasing melancholy association between evil and dreams. . . . Coleridge had now every reason to dread the terrifying activity of the unconscious."[41] But he was never able to say that the imagination was a power of terror as well as of delight.[†]

Indeed *Hamlet* does not move "in the sunlight," as Eliot says, it is stuck in the subjective dark. But it is about being

---

*". . . or the startling *hysteric* of weakness over-exerting itself."—BL II, 85.

†"Rarely in the poems and never in the later theoretical writing is there an openly acknowledged *fear* of the imagination."—Walter Jackson Bate, *Coleridge* (1968), 109.

stuck in the dark. Both Coleridge and Eliot were afraid of the dark of subjectivity. Coleridge told his fear, over and over; that is what his Hamlet theory and so much else in his life and thought are about. Eliot the doctrinaire repudiated the fear that Eliot the man of modern sensibility felt at his nerve ends, by treating subjective darkness as a moral and aesthetic and religious failure, a modern heresy. "Those of us who find ourselves supporting . . . Classicism [he wrote in 1923 in "The Function of Criticism"] believe that men cannot get on without giving allegiance to something outside themselves." Eliot's militancy, in life and literature, sprang from his fear of sinking down and down into himself, without anything outside to catch hold of; against the *Hamlet* darkness around him he beat a hollow-sounding antique drum.

But not to the bitter end. In 1955, on the occasion of his being awarded the Goethe Prize at Hamburg University, an easier-minded man talked not about *Hamlet* the "artistic failure" but about Hamlet the "European symbol" and "European myth-hero."[42] That symbolic Hamlet is of course the one who is lost in the darkness of his own self. And for English-speaking people he is first of all Coleridge's Hamlet.

Coleridge portrays Hamlet as somebody who is spellbound by his own inwardness; he notes "the aversion to externals," the "habit of brooding over the world within him"—"that aversion to action" and "retiring from reality, which is the result of having, what we express by the terms, a world within himself."[43] This describes a species of introvert. Psychologically, it is simplistic, for it leaves out of account, as Bradley says, the Hamlet who is "apt to be decided and even imperious if thwarted or interfered with," Freud's "callous Renaissance prince." However, what looks like psychological simplism is really philosophical generality. In discovering an extreme of "intellectual activity" opposed to an extreme "aversion to real action" in Hamlet,[44] Coleridge is inexplicitly recognizing, beneath the particular psychological type he sketches, a general (metaphysical) antagonism between the self and the world. This division in the primary constitution of things, this split between thinking and acting, inwardness and outwardness, subject and object, underlies the diversity of psychological types and the complexity of individual psyches—underlies, that is, the entire psychological reality. But it comes to *consciousness* in the *self*-consciousness of the introverted psychological type of the modern artist and the artist-protagonist he models after himself in his work.

Hamlet is not yet a Coleridge, he is still a Renaissance prince, though one who is tied in knots. Coleridge is not yet an Underground Man or a Tonio Kröger. But Coleridge sees in Hamlet what the Underground Man, later in the century, sees in himself: an "overacute consciousness" which separates him from the "men of action," the "people who know how to revenge themselves," and turns him into a "mouse"; what Tonio Kröger sees in himself in the next century: a soul "eaten up with intellect and introspection."

Seeing Coleridge's own face through the features of his Hamlet does not mean seeing *through* Coleridge's Hamlet. Hazlitt wrote a cruel essay on the poet-philosopher in *The Spirit of the Age*, yet he does him justice here. "Mr. Coleridge talks of himself, without being an egotist, for in him the individual is always merged in the abstract and general." Coleridge took a sneaking pride in the resemblance he found between himself and Hamlet, which did not go unnoticed. Crabb Robinson, after hearing the 1812 lecture, commented in his diary on the "striking observations on the virtue of action and the futility of talents that divert from rather than lead to action. I doubt whether he did not design that an application should be made to himself, and whether he is not well content to meet the censure of his own remarks, for the sake of the reputation of those talents apparently depreciated." [45]

Yet we know that Coleridge was *not* content to make that bargain—to enjoy the reputation of a Hamlet brilliance of mind at the cost of his life as a man. His Hamletism was a life-stifling oppression that he longed to understand and cast off; as narcissistically dear as his own self was to him, so repulsive was it too.

Now and then, it is true, "S. T. C." gets in his way instead of pointing the way; there is an interfering vicariousness. Coleridge misses wildly when he describes Hamlet as "running away from the *particular* into the *general*. This aversion to personal, individual concerns, and escape to generalizations and general reasonings a most important characteristic." [46] Hamlet is a generalizer but not an escapist generalizer; there is no such tendency to self-evasion in his discourses. What Coleridge is describing is his own "dejected" self, whose "sole resource" and "only plan" for escaping from his "afflictions" (as he puts it in *Dejection*) was "not to think of what I needs must feel":

> For not to think of what I needs must feel,
>   But to be still and patient, all I can;
> And haply by abstruse research to steal
>   From my own nature all the natural man—
>   This was my sole resource, my only plan:
> Till that which suits the part infects the whole,
> And now is almost grown the habit of my soul.

Coleridge—as just this quotation and the one above, about Hamlet escaping from himself into generalizations, imply—was not afraid of self and self-interest as a deceiving bias in his ideas; he was afraid of the *loss* of self in his ideas.

One excellence of the Doctrine of Plato, or of the Plotino-platonic Philosophy, is that it never suffers, much less causes or even occasions, its Disciples to forget themselves, lost and scattered in sensible Objects disjoined or *as* disjoined from themselves. It is

impossible to understand the Elements of this Philosophy without an appeal, at every step & round of the Ladder, to the fact
within, to the mind's consciousness.[47]

He was a thinker who all his life pursued the universal in the
particular. The smack of Hamlet that he found in himself revealed to him a universal condition: the Hamlet condition of
the modern self struggling with as much ignominiousness as
brilliance—with a glittering ignominiousness, as it were—
against the paralyzing disunion of reflective mind and effective will, spirituality and vitality. In all the books and essays
of *Hamlet* criticism which have poured like a flood since Coleridge's day, the implicit reach of his conception has never
really been exceeded because it is coextensive with the play as
a European myth-symbol.

The "subjectivity" of Coleridge's Hamlet, as of all his
thought, is strength, not weakness. "There have been men in
all ages," he wrote, "who have been impelled as by an instinct
to propose their own nature as a problem, and who devote
their attempts to its solution."[48] He was one of those who proposed his own nature as a problem; he was brave enough to
try to study the problem of himself. Out of that attempt came,
among other things, his theory of Hamlet. The maxim he
was always proclaiming was, Know thyself!—"the heaven-
descended [commandment to] KNOW THYSELF!"[49] The essence
of man's nature, he said, lies in his "reflex consciousness,"*
his consciousness of self. Self-knowledge is the way in which
men realize their essential nature. Yet many avert their eyes
from themselves: "Surely, there is a strange—nay, rather a too
natural—aversion in many to know themselves."[50] Hamlet is
not one of these. Coleridge praises him for being "deeply ac-

---

*"For Reflexion seems the first approach to, & shadow of, the divine Perma-
nency; the first effort of divine working in us to bind the Past and Future with
the Present, and thereby to let in upon us some faint glimmering of that State
in which Past, Present, and Future are co-adunated in the adorable I AM."—
CL II, 1197.

quainted with his own feelings" and "painting them with such wonderful power and accuracy," for "having a perfect knowledge of his own character"—even though that character is "so weak as to be unable to carry into act his most obvious duty."[51] Coleridge too is one of those who tries to know himself; Mrs. Coleridge, on the other hand, is not. His wife's mind, he writes to Robert Southey on July 29, 1802,

> in all disputes uniformly *projects* itself *forth* to recriminate, instead of turning itself inward with a silent Self-questioning. Our virtues & our vices are exact antitheses—I so attentively watch my own Nature, that my worst Self-delusion is, a compleat Self-knowledge, so mixed with intellectual complacency, that my quickness to see & readiness to acknowledge my faults is too often frustrated by the small pain, which the sight of them gives me, & the consequent slowness to amend them. Mrs. C. is so stung by the very first thought of being in the wrong that she never amends because she never endures to look at her own mind at all, in it's [*sic*] faulty parts—but shelters herself from painful Self-enquiry by angry Recrimination.[52]

But there is an anomaly in what he says about himself and Hamlet as self-knowers. Hamlet knows his own character perfectly, and yet perfect self-knowledge does not bring with it the "practical" power to perform even "his most obvious duty." Coleridge's near-perfect self-knowledge is also helpless; he sees his own faults clearly but still he doesn't mend them. *Self-knowledge is impotent.* Indeed it *makes* you impotent: if you study to know yourself too well, the very effort of self-study lands you in the Hamlet fix, in that "over-balance in the contemplative faculty" in which "man becomes a creature of meditation, and loses the power of action."[53] The reason for this impotence of self-knowledge (as Coleridge concluded bitterly at the end of his life) is: self-knowledge is only the knowledge of the mystery of the self, not the knowledge that would dispel the mystery. Where man's nature is unknown, self-knowledge is only the knowledge of the mystery of man's nature.

This impotence of the self-conscious mind, of a mind, like Hamlet's, lost in meditation on itself—

> *Polonius.*   You know sometimes he walks four hours together
> Here in the lobby
>
> (II.ii.160)

—is not the same thing as the innocent impracticality of the man of learning, the unworldly clerk. Goethe's Hamlet, not Coleridge's, is an unworldly idealist fresh from the academic groves of Wittenberg; overwhelmed by the revelation of the evil of the world, his slender, pale-faced innocence caves in under the weight of his murderous duty.* Coleridge's Hamlet is not weak from book study but from self-study. Though he too is an idealist (Hamlet's speech about the wassail music, Coleridge says, "so finely reveal[s] the predominant idealism, the ratiocinative meditativeness of his character"[54]), his is an idealism of knowing, not of unworldly not-knowing, of "ratiocinative meditativeness." It consists in a literally "idealistic" brooding over the ideas in his own head, over "the world within him." His kind of "idealism" is pathological rather than naive. "Such a mind as Hamlet's is near akin to madness" because, "unseated from its healthy balance, [it] is for ever occupied with the world within him, and abstracted from external things; his words give a substance to shadows, and he is dissatisfied with commonplace realities."[55] There is not in Hamlet "a due balance between the real and the imaginary world." His "thoughts, images, fancy"—all the teeming contents of his poet-philosopher's head—are "far more vivid" to him "than his perceptions" of the external world; indeed "his

---

*"A beautiful, pure, noble and most moral nature sinks beneath a burden which it can neither bear nor cast off."—*Wilhelm Meister's Apprenticeship,* Chap. 13.

very perceptions," because they are instantly "pass[ed] thro' the medium of his contemplations . . . acquir[e] as they pass a form and color not naturally their own. Hence great, enormous, intellectual activity, and a consequent proportionate aversion to real action."[56]

Although Coleridge emphasizes that Hamlet's "aversion to real action" is the direct consequence of his introverted intellectuality, it is by no means clear why this should be so. "Act," writes Auden,

> from thought should quickly follow.
> What is thinking for?

Why should thinking, which would seem to be a first or proto-movement, arrest all movement, in Hamlet's (and Coleridge's*) case? *Why*, for introspective and meditative temperaments, should the external world of things and acts lose in reality and wither away to a shadow? That the activity of reason should have in it a pathological possibility, that reason itself should thus prove unreasonable—this was an unprecedented thing. Coleridge perhaps comes closest to a psychological *explanation* of Hamlet—as distinct from a *description*—in "The Character of Hamlet," where he comments on the soliloquy beginning "O that this too too solid† flesh . . .":

> The reasons why *taedium vitae* oppresses minds like Hamlet's:
> the exhaustion of bodily feeling from perpetual exertion of mind;
> that all mental form being indefinite and ideal, realities must

---

*Of course he is talking about himself equally with Hamlet. See also his January 1802 letter to Godwin: "Partly from ill-health, & partly from an unhealthy & reverie-like vividness of *Thoughts*, & (pardon the pedantry of the phrase) a diminished Impressibility from *Things*, my ideas, wishes & feelings are to a diseased degree disconnected from *motion & action*."—CL II, 782.

†The now-favored reading of *sullied* would not have deterred Coleridge from seeing solid life-reality and indefinite mind-ideality at war in *Hamlet*.

needs become cold, and hence it is the indefinite that combines with passion.[57]

This is quite elliptical. But a notebook entry of November 1810, about "the *thinking* disease," throws light on it:

> The *thinking* disease, in which feelings instead of embodying themselves in *acts* ascend, & become materials of general reasoning & intellectual pride.—The dreadful consequences of this *perversion*, instanced in Germany, Fichte versus Kant, Schelling versus Fichte—and alas! in Verbidegno [Wordsworth] versus [S.T.C.].—Ascent where Nature meant Descent—and thus shortening the process—viz—*feelings* made the Subjects & tangible substance of Thought, instead of Actions, Realizations, *things* done & as such externalized & *remembered*. On such meagre Diet as (feelings evaporated) embryos interrupted in their progress to *Birth*, no moral Being ever became healthy.[58]

Life becomes an oppression to "minds like Hamlet's" because their unnaturally hypertrophic mental being absorbs all their affect and leaves them drained and depleted in their human being; the effect of their passions detaching themselves from the substantial realities of their bodily existences and attaching themselves to the indefinite idealities of their minds—"Ascent where Nature meant Descent"—is to leave them in an attenuated, spectral state of disliking enervation—more ghosts than men. The essential idea here is Coleridge's often-expressed one of an unbalancing of Hamlet's character toward inwardness and ideality and away from "outness" and reality. This is accompanied, however, by a suggestion of something more psychologically concrete: of a syndrome in the psychosomatic economy whereby the vital energies proper to bodily realities are diverted (perverted) from their natural objects and expended on objects of the mind. What we have here is a metapsychological recognition of the loss of vitality which has accompanied the intellectualization of life, of Hamletism as a general condition.

Coleridge ignores the fact that Hamlet expressly declares

that his moral revulsion against the world is prompted by his revulsion against his mother's speed in remarrying. In the same way, he refuses to take seriously Hamlet's expressed motive for sparing the King when he finds him praying—that he wishes to kill Claudius when he is "about some act / That has no relish of salvation in't." (III.iii.92). He interprets Hamlet's pulling back not as horrible implacability but as "reluctance and procrastination." All his feeling is for the omnipotence of psychological tendency in Hamlet, all his insistence is on *Hamlet* as a tragedy of the self in bondage to itself. To take declared motives and concerns seriously while the self remained in all its inveteracy was simplemindedness—Coleridge exclaims against "the folly of all motive-mongering, while the individual self remains."[59]

But because of this very psychologism, which represented such an advance over the older criticism, Coleridge misunderstands what he calls, quite inexactly, Hamlet's *tedium vitae*. He equates this with his own gray state of passionless, benumbed inanition, a state which is like that of

> a becalmèd bark,
> Whose Helmsman on an ocean waste and wide
> Sits mute and pale his mouldering helm beside.
>
> *(Constancy to an Ideal Object)*

Describing the "complete *tedium vitae*" from which his friend and patron Thomas Wedgwood suffered, Coleridge says, "Life in all its forms move, in his diseased moments, like shadows before him, cold, colourless, and unsubstantial."[60]

Hamlet, however, isn't *apathetically* weary of the world, he loathes and contemns it; it fills him with disgust and nausea. Coleridge has little feeling for the element of free, impassioned judgment in Hamlet's rejection of the world, for Hamlet the world-hater. He himself never really rejected the world, worldly though he found it. The Pantisocratic scheme of establishing a colony on the banks of the Susquehanna had been the product of his young enthusiasm, not of any world hatred. He was always very respectful toward—indeed stood in awe of—men highly placed in the world (as he himself said). From the start, the worldly world gave him trouble; it was hard for him to get along in it. He tried to appease it, ingratiate himself with it, dazzle it with brilliant talk. He did not positively reject it and it did not positively reject him, even though he felt himself an outsider in so many ways, an "Alien in the World of Worldlings."[61] Contempt for the world like Hamlet's is bound up with a ferocious self-condemnation, with a moral despair of oneself as well as the world—and the closer Coleridge felt himself coming to moral despair of the world and himself, the more he shrank from such despair in terror, taking refuge in his Christian piety.

The *energy* of Hamlet's negative feelings, his life- and world-disgust, is untraditional, unreligious, uncondoned. In the "To be or not to be" soliloquy, it leads to a quite strange confusion of death and defeat with eager, positive actions: at the end of the speech Hamlet has insensibly passed over to talking about suicide as if it were a bold and vigorous undertaking, one of the "enterprises of great pitch and moment." There is a touch of the sinister about this, as there is a touch of the sinister about Hamlet in general. Coleridge says nothing about this sinister aspect of the soliloquy, this element of "positive Negation" in Hamlet. Yet it was a threatening presence in his own life and thought. *Positive Negation* is his own term. The culminating phrase in the tortuous and tortured poem *Limbo*, it distinguishes "growthless, dull Privation"—*tedium vitae*, his own limbo state of death-in-life—from a worse fate:

> A lurid thought is growthless, dull Privation,
> Yet that is but a Purgatory curse;
> Hell knows a fear far worse,
> A fear—a future state;—'tis positive Negation!

In *Ne Plus Ultra*, a poem which followed on the heels of *Limbo*, positive negation is called the "one permitted opposite of God." But as the

> sole despair
> Of both th' eternities in Heaven!
> Sole interdict of all bedewing prayer,

it threatens to overwhelm God and Heaven. * Coleridge hoped for life-in-death through Christ, after his limbo years of death-in-life on earth. Positive negation threatened this only hope left to him, his religious hope. The phrase expresses from the side of his despair, in a poem, what he more often tries to express from the side of religious hopefulness, in prose: his sense of Being—*his* being—as a struggle against an armed and active Nonbeing. (His despair exclaimed in poetry; his hope argued in prose.)

In the end, of course, Coleridge can't explain Hamlet, he can only describe him. I say "of course" because surely we know now, after so many explanations, that there is no explanation—meaning by *explanation* the elucidation of some basic psychological mechanism or disposition or fundamental moral or religious motive. The art of Shakespeare in this play begins and ends with Hamlet's inexplicability. The protagonist discovered to us is a Hamlet in chains, a Hamlet who never stops crying, "I do not know / Why yet I live to say, 'This thing's to do' . . ." (IV.iv.43). From beginning to end, he is never able to do "this thing"; what he finally does is bring the roof down on himself and everyone. If a work of art is a concrete universal, then Hamlet's impotence falls on his universal side, the side of his philosophical generality, not on the side of his psychological concreteness. But because he is painted with such incomparable fullness of being we seem to see him

---

* "O Wedding-Guest! this soul hath been
  Alone on a wide wide sea!
  So lonely 'twas, that God himself
  Scarce seemèd there to be."

in a perspective that reaches beyond the five acts of the play, beyond the artifice of art, into the shadowy psychological depths of a concrete living soul—but that is only the depth illusion of great realistic art.

Hamlet is the tragedy of a self which has become inexplicable to itself, a self in rebellion against its own inherited self-understanding—a self Shakespeare treats on the same level with himself as the playwright and not from the superior height of knowledge *(de haut en bas)* from which he treats his other tragic heroes. *[62] With Shakespeare's other heroes we always know, looking down from the height we share with the author, what the real case is; in the case of Hamlet, playwright and audience know no more, essentially, than the character knows. To know Hamlet better than he knows himself, to know him *de haut en bas*, no longer belongs to the traditional prerogatives and powers of an author but is an arrogant pretension against which Hamlet defends himself with near-hysterical indignation. After pressing the recorder on Guildenstern, who backs away protesting he doesn't know the stops, Hamlet shouts "how unworthy a thing" Guildenstern would make of him by seeming to know *his* stops: "Why, look you now, how unworthy a thing you would make of me! You would play upon me, you would seem to know my stops, you would pluck out the heart of my mystery, you would sound me from my lowest note to the top of my compass. . . . 'Sblood, do you think I am easier to be played on than a pipe?" (III.ii.349). Here Hamlet is jealously defending the living mystery of himself against all soul-managers and soul-explainers who would make an unworthy thing of him.

To explain Hamlet would be to pluck out the heart of his mystery, which is to say his tragedy, for his mystery *is* his tragedy. The best criticism of *Hamlet* strengthens our feeling

---

*"None of us [today], no matter what our situation, really knows the form of the plot he is in, and Hamlet was the first theatrical figure who expressed this fact fully."—Lionel Abel, *Metatheatre* (1963), 58.

for the mystery and the elements which make up the mystery; it does not make the mystery disappear. Freud's theory of Shakespeare's play is valuable for the way in which it deepens our appreciation of the depths of inwardness in Hamlet, who is convulsed by an unknown struggle. But as a complicated speculation about how Hamlet is unable to "take vengeance on the man who did away with his father and took that father's place with his mother," because Claudius only "shows him the repressed wishes of his own childhood realized,"[63] it is about to turn into a Rube Goldberg cartoon of crazy connections. *Hamlet* serves Freud's idea, the idea doesn't serve the play. Freud's idea doesn't love the play, it loves itself.

After a lifetime of studying Shakespeare and himself, Coleridge had the same explanation for himself and Hamlet that he started out with as a young man: "weak character." He hadn't solved "the Hamlet problem" as he liked to think he had, and of course he never solved "the Coleridge problem." But he hadn't gotten nowhere. Thanks to his efforts it became possible to understand the play (and himself) as the psycho-philosophical tragedy of the I AM (ego) of the modern spirit in oppugnant division from the IT IS (id) of the world—not a simple, separate world opposed to a simple, separate self, but an It which is in the I and an I which is in the It, yet sundered. This idea of the disjunctive involution of the one in the other—to express it in Coleridgian style—points straight ahead to the most serious efforts of modern times to understand the mystery of man's nature.

During 1808–1810, Coleridge lived on and off for nearly two years with the Wordsworths at Allan Bank in Grasmere. A man miserable in body and soul, he made that uncomfortable house even more uncomfortable for his friends by his difficult presence; the upshot of the long cohabitation was the rupture of the friendship between the two men. However, intellectual activity ("abstruse research") was always Coleridge's refuge from his troubles; and it was while living at Allan Bank that he wrote and published his periodical *The Friend, A Weekly Essay*. When he announced the venture, those who knew him best expected least from it—expected nothing. Lamb wrote to Hazlitt: "There came this morning a printed prospectus from S. T. Coleridge, Grasmere, of a weekly paper, to be called *The Friend*. . . . There came also a notice of a turkey from Mr. Clarkson, which I am more sanguine in expecting the accomplishment of than I am of Coleridge's prophecy." Just before the first number appeared on June 1, 1809, Wordsworth wrote exasperatedly to Coleridge's and his old friend Thomas Poole (May 30, 1809):

> I am sorry to say that nothing appears to me more desirable than that his periodical essay should never commence. It is in fact *impossible* utterly impossible—that he should carry it on. . . . I give it to you as my deliberate opinion . . . that he neither can nor will execute any thing of important benefit either to himself his family or mankind. Neither his talents nor his genius mighty as they are nor his vast information will avail him anything; they are all frustrated by a derangement in his intellectual and moral constitution—In fact he has no voluntary power of mind whatsoever, nor is he capable of acting under any *constraint* of duty or moral obligation. Do not suppose that I mean to say from this that The Friend may not appear—it may—but it cannot go on for any length of time. I am *sure* it cannot. . . . The disease of his mind is that he perpetually looks out of himself for those obstacles to his utility which exist only in himself. . . . Pray burn this letter when you have read it.

Coleridge, however, confounded his friends by putting out some twenty-seven numbers of *The Friend*, doing what Wordsworth had said it was "utterly impossible" for him to do. Yet the prospectus which had announced his plan to publish the periodical had not been encouraging. As much an apology as a promise, the prospectus confessed that "the Number of my unrealized Schemes, and the Mass of my miscellaneous Fragments, have often furnished my Friends with a Subject of

Raillery, and sometimes of Regret and Reproof." He blamed his "Want of Perseverance" in realizing his schemes on his Hamletism: "Over-activity of Thought, modified by a constitutional Indolence, which made it more pleasant to me to continue acquiring [that is, to go on reading], than to reduce what I had acquired to a regular Form."[64] It is of course true that Coleridge loved his library, loved wild weather outside and the firelight playing on the backs of his "dear Books" within,[65] yet the pleasure he took in endless reading was equally a form of dread. In the very next sentence in his prospectus he describes his dread, a kind of obsession (which he calls a "conviction")—his "Conviction, that, in Order fully to comprehend and develope any one Subject, it was necessary that I should make myself Master of some other, which again as regularly involved a third, and so on, with an ever-widening Horizon." This industrious indolence—indolence because the endless industry of preparation was a form of postponement—this dread that less than all should prove to be no more than nothing, was however turned to account by the activity of his mind in "almost daily throwing off . . . Notices or Reflections in desultory Fragments"—by his habit "of daily noting down in my Memorandum or Common-place Books, both Incidents and Observations; whatever had occurred to me from without, and all the Flux and Reflux of my Mind within itself. The Number of these Notices, and their Tendency, miscellaneous as they were, to one common End . . . first encouraged me to undertake the Weekly Essay."[66]

In other words: in spite of his bad record he had some confidence that he could realize *this* scheme of an essay periodical because it suited the nature of his mind "both in its Strength and in its Weakness" (as he put it in the next sentence). Its weakness was its desultoriness and running to fragments; its strength was that the fragments tended "to one common End." Here in the prospectus he accepted the fact that he was unable to erect grand architectures of finished thought— epics of philosophy, as it were—and went on to write *The*

Friend, the *Biographia Literaria* after it, and the other works of his latter years, all of them miscellanies only tending toward unity. But he did not *really* accept this fact about himself. Some years before, in 1804, during the voyage out to Malta, he had written in his notebook: "—I have many thoughts, many images; large Stores of the unwrought materials; scarcely a day passes but something new in fact or in illustration rises up in me, like Herbs and Flowers in a Garden in early Spring; but the combining Power, the power to do, the manly effective *Will*, that is dead or slumbers most diseasedly." [67] He was perforce a fragmentist and writer of miscellanies because the "manly effective" will which would have combined his materials into substantial finished works slept "diseasedly" in him. And so, though he confounded Wordsworth's prediction by producing twenty-seven numbers of *The Friend*, Coleridge himself still agreed with him that he had "no voluntary power of mind," that he was incapable of "acting under any *constraint* of duty," especially his duty to his own genius.

The call of duty stunned him rather than roused him, he said. [68] His "way-ward and desultory" genius could not "brook a task-master! The tenderest touch from the hand of *Obligation* wounds thee, like a scourge of Scorpions!" [69] Duty was something that threatened him from without; if only it were a free ebullition from within! One of his earliest notebook entries, going back to 1795–96, reads: "What we *must* do, let us love to do. It is a noble Chemistry, that turns Necessity into Pleasure!" [70] This longing to unite necessity and pleasure, obligation and inclination, moral law and natural impulse was born out of Coleridge's sense of his own weakness; but it was as a young revolutionary feeling the wind of world redemption blowing from across the Channel that he dared to hope for such a union. In the Republic of Love (Fraternity) there was no need for policemen, nor the Policeman Duty armed with "a rod / To check the erring, and reprove," as Wordsworth, feeling the responsibilities of a family man after two years of marriage, put it in his *Ode to Duty* in 1804. (In 1798 one impulse from a vernal wood taught you more morality than all the sages could; in 1804 Wordsworth downgraded natural impulse to "chance-desires" which needed the strict control of law.) Coleridge quarrelled with Wordsworth's "Stern Lawgiver" because she seemed stern; later on he quarrelled with Wordsworth because Wordsworth seemed stern and judged so harshly the friend who had always loved him. He quarrelled, too, with Kant because the Categorical Imperative was stern, wearing, he thought, an expression that was minatory, not amiable. Where there was not the smile of affection beaming down on him he could do nothing!

As a kind of rebuttal to Wordsworth's *Ode to Duty*, Coleridge thought of writing "an Ode to Pleasure." Thus he would be defending against his friend the principle his friend had upheld so boldly in the 1800 preface to the *Lyrical Ballads* and had then turned away from, submitting to a new control: the principle of nature in which Wordsworth had found "the native and naked dignity of man" to consist, "the grand elementary principle of pleasure, by which he knows, and feels, and lives, and moves." But Coleridge never wrote the ode— which is no great loss. It would have been a feeble, nervously defensive effort, for he did not mean to allow pleasure anything as pleasure, only as it promoted virtue: "An Ode to Pleasure—not sought for herself, but as the conditio sine qua non of virtuous activity."[71] Coleridge was a guilty man all his life; but after opium got hold of him he became a helpless prisoner of his guilt and always had to show, to others and to himself, that all his faults and failures and especially his bondage to opium had "been the consequence of some Dread or other on my mind / from fear of Pain, or Shame, not from prospect of Pleasure."[72]

Wordsworth said in his letter to Poole that "the disease of [Coleridge's] mind is that he perpetually looks out of himself for those obstacles to his utility which exist only in himself."

He meant Coleridge was always finding excuses. But we know from Coleridge's notebooks how much he accused himself to himself, as well as excused himself. There is a notebook passage where he catches himself putting off a duty and takes himself to task about it. He should have been reading and annotating Malthus' essay on population, he writes on January 9, 1804 (apparently because he had promised Southey to help him write a review of the work):

> I had begun & found it pleasant / why did I neglect it?—Because, I OUGHT not to have done this.—The same in reading & writing Letters, Essays, &c &c—surely this is well worth a serious Analysis, that understanding I may attempt to heal / for it is a deep & wide disease in my moral Nature, at once Elm-and-Oak-rooted.—Love of Liberty, Pleasure of Spontaneity, &c &c, these all express, not explain, the Fact.

However, when he got into bed that night he found that he had been "pompously" treating as a problem something whose solution was obvious. The whole thing was to be explained by association. From infancy up we are used to "Parents, Schoolmasters, Tutors, Inspectors, &c" interrupting our "self-chosen Pursuits" and telling us what to do. Now duty too is a command, though one we lay on ourselves. But by association with the commands imposed on us from without during the period of our tutelage, it calls up sensations of pain and reluctance.

So Coleridge analyzed the matter. But at half-past-one in the morning he awoke and found his solution false. No, it wasn't the case that the idea of duty became associated with painful feelings. It was rather that the imperative of duty was painful by its very nature and not by association; it was an abrupt breaking in on, a curbing of the natural tendency of the mind, so strong in natures like his own and his son Hartley's, to drift indolently on the current of itself:

> *Interruption* of itself is painful because & as far as it acts as Disruption / & then, without any reference to . . . my former theory,

I saw great Reason to attribute the effect wholly to the streamy
nature of the associating Faculty and especially as it is evident
that *they most* labor under this defect who are most reverie-ish
& streamy — Hartley, for instance & myself / This seems to me
no common corroboration of my former Thought on the origin of
moral Evil in general.[73]

He was a mental drifter who lacked the firmness of mind and
concentration of purpose he saw so strongly displayed, to his
own shame, in the character of his best friend.

The "former Thought" on evil to which he refers is a speculation in which his own reverie-ish and streamy self is written large as a general theory: he tries to explain "the Origin of
moral Evil from the *streamy* Nature of Association, which
Thinking-Reason, curbs & rudders." That is, without the rudder of reason to steer the mind, the dangerous currents of
association sweep it headlong into evil thoughts. "Do not," he
asks, "the bad Passions in Dreams throw light & shew of
proof upon this Hypothesis?"—that is, does not the fact that
the mind rages and lusts in dreams when the helmsman reason is off duty seem to offer proof of his theory? "Explain
those bad Passions: and I shall gain Light, I am sure—A Clue!
A Clue!" But then he wonders if the innocence of children or
the innocence of tranquil sleep does not contradict his hypothesis, for in childhood and in peaceful sleep there is no
ruddering reason either. The upshot of his speculation is that
"as far as I can see anything in this Total Mist, Vice is im-
perfect . . . Volition, giving diseased Currents of association. . . ."[74] "Diseased Currents of association" are unmas-
tered thoughts and impulses, the "bad Passions in Dreams"
—the spontaneous and uncontrolled arising out of unconsciousness. The unconscious, which he said is the genius in
the man of genius ("There is in genius itself an unconscious
activity; nay, that is *the* genius in the man of genius."),[75] is the
source of evil *and* of genius. Out of the uncontrolled come
both the grandeur of genius and the misery of moral evil.

Coleridge's Hamletism, which he defined as a falling into

desuetude and dryness of the natural man from too much metaphysics and mind, here plainly shows itself, underneath its passive surface, as a tense ambivalence, a straining deadlock. He fears spontaneity, impulsiveness, the ebullition and unruddered streaming of feelings, thoughts, imaginations as the source of evil; and he loves them as the stuff of life. This ambivalence belongs to the fundamental structure of his self-division. Coleridge loved the pantheistic all, the organic whole, nature and natural impulsiveness, Spinoza, Wordsworth—and he feared them. On its psychological side, his Christianity is a recoil from this love; it falls, psychologically, on the side of his fear rather than his love.

Coleridge's intellect was fertile in devising formulas and phrases to reconcile the antagonistic importunities of duty and desire, law and impulse, thought and life; but his being could not follow his intellect. "What is Music?" he asked— "Passion and order aton'd! Imperative Power in Obedience!"[76] His own passions, however, remained disordered, his own powers disobedient to his will. What is poetry? he asked, always answering to the effect that it was a "balance or reconciliation of opposite or discordant qualities."[77] During the voyage to Malta in the spring of 1804, when sea and shipboard made *The Ancient Mariner* live again in his feelings, and when his own feelings of guilt and dread made sea and shipboard live for him as they do in his poem, he called poetry "a rationalized dream dealing . . . to manifold Forms our own Feelings, that never perhaps were attached by us consciously to our own personal Selves."[78] Poetry is a wildly working dream disciplined into sense by the rationalizing imagination, an anarchy of buried feelings raised into lucidity and order by being externalized in objective forms. "What is the Lear, the Othello," the entry continues, "but a divine Dream / all Shakespere, & nothing Shakespere." But Coleridge himself was able to write great poetry—that is, raise his deepest affective life up into the light of some kind of conscious poetic contemplation—only for the briefest time.

Poetry was a rationalized dream, and more particularly it was a rationalized nightmare, not only for the author of *The Ancient Mariner* but for Shakespeare also, as Coleridge's reference to those nightmarish tragedies *Lear* and *Othello* suggests. Poetry was a wrestling with "the frightful fiend." In *The Ancient Mariner*, in the first part of the abortive *Christabel*, and in a certain sense in *Kubla Khan* as well, Coleridge entered into his nightmares and wrestled with his demon. His sleep was tormented by terrors all his life; but the hope and strength or whatever it was he needed to grapple with them he possessed only during some few months in 1797–98, when his friendship with Wordsworth was in its first, exultant stage. Whatever else *The Ancient Mariner* is, it is a poem about guilt and fear and horror, shame and remorse and awful loneliness of soul—not contemplated by the poet from some remove but felt directly in the very midst of the nightmare turmoil. In *The Ancient Mariner* Coleridge took seriously his nightmare terrors; he wrestled with "the Fiend." Before and after his miraculous short term of greatness, however, he strove "to keep the Fiend at Arm's length," as he put it in a letter to his brother in October 1803:

> While I am awake, & retain possession of my Will & Reason, I can contrive to keep the Fiend at Arm's length; but Sleep throws wide open all the Gates of the beleaguered City—& such an Host of Horrors rush in—that three nights out of four I fall asleep struggling to lie awake, and start up & bless my own loud Screams, that have awakened me.[79]

This letter dates from a period—the fall and winter of 1803–1804—when his nights were so horror-haunted that he dreaded to fall asleep. In another letter from the same time, writing about his physical sufferings, he says, "The Horrors of my Sleep, and Night-screams . . . seemed to carry beyond mere Body—counterfeiting, as it were, the Tortures of Guilt, and what we are told of the Punishments of a spiritual World." He is now a convalescent, he continues, "but dreading such another Bout as much as I dare dread a Thing which has no immediate connection with my Conscience."[80] His repudiation here of the moral significance of his dreams shows so much awareness of their moral significance that you suspect him of being disingenuous. But who is to say where disingenuousness left off in him and genuine inconscience began?

In a notebook entry made aboard the *Speedwell* as it carried him to Malta, the same entry in which he proposed an ode to pleasure, Coleridge describes his sleep as "a pandemonium of all the shames & miseries of the past Life from early childhood all huddled together, & bronzed with one stormy Light of Terror & Self-torture."[81] This sentence, with its violent nightmare vividness describing a soul driven hard before the storm blasts of its conscience, seems a clear enough acknowledgment on Coleridge's part of the moral significance of his dreams. Perhaps such an acknowledgment came more easily to him under circumstances which recalled his poem about the tormented Mariner—that figure of truth from the depths of his emotional life.

Coleridge was an introspectionist who fled in terror from what his deepest self-inspection might reveal. His "peccatum originale," he wrote in 1828, might be expressed as, among other things, "mental Cowardice of whatever might force my attention to myself."[82] In 1822 he wrote to Thomas Allsop that his "eloquence was most commonly excited by the desire of running away and hiding myself from my personal & inward feelings, and not for the expression of them. . . . I fled in a circle still overtaken by the Feelings, from which I was evermore fleeing, with my back turned toward them. . . ."[83] This seems much the same as what he had said two decades before in *Dejection*, that his "sole resource" and "only plan" was "not to think of what [he] needs must feel" but to bury himself in "abstruse research" instead. But what had earlier been called a "plan" is now, in the last decade of life, condemned as "mental Cowardice."

The feelings Coleridge accuses himself of averting his attention from were those painful ones excited in him by the afflictions and defeats of his life. But lying behind those painful feelings which he knew too well but did not wish to think about, pressing against the barrier walls of his consciousness, was an obscure mass of painful fears and impulses which he did *not* know, which he *feared* to know; and those feelings too—those especially—he did not wish to think about. In the letter to Allsop, he speaks about fleeing "in a circle still overtaken by the Feelings, from which I was evermore fleeing, with my back turned toward them." This sounds scared and recalls the Ancient Mariner looking out, in Part VI, on the green ocean but afraid to see what is there:

> Like one, that on a lonesome road
> Doth walk in fear and dread,
> And having once turned round walks on,
> And turns no more his head;
> Because he knows, a frightful fiend
> Doth close behind him tread.

In *The Ancient Mariner* Coleridge does not repudiate the terrors of his inner life as having no moral connection with himself; he does not ask plaintively, as he would later ask in his poem *The Pains of Sleep*, why the Fiend should pick on him. In the person of the Mariner he accepts his fears, and his fear of his fears, and produces in the quoted stanza, whose alternation of forward movement and arrest is the very kinesthesia of terror, one of the nakedest evocations of dread in all literature.

What scared Coleridge so? What was the frightful fiend he fled from with averted eyes? The violent, overwhelming middle stanza of *The Pains of Sleep*, which describes the emotional contents of his nightmares from the outside, from the side of his shaken consciousness, provides a kind of catalogue of the "Shapes & Thoughts that tortur'd" him, though in general terms only, without specifying concretely what the shapes and thoughts were:*

> Desire with Loathing strangely mixt,
> On wild or hateful Objects fixt:
> Pangs of Revenge, the powerless Will,
> Still baffled, & consuming still,
> Sense of intolerable Wrong,
> And men whom I despis'd made strong
> Vain-glorious Threats, unmanly Vaunting,
> Bad men my boasts & fury taunting
> Rage, sensual Passion, mad'ning Brawl,
> And Shame, and Terror over all!
> Deeds to be hid that were not hid,
> Which, all confus'd I might not know,
> Whether I suffer'd or I did:
> For all was Horror, Guilt & Woe,
> My own or others, still the same,
> Life-stifling Fear, Soul-stifling Shame!

In the poem's last stanza he sums up this catalogue of rage and fear, lust and shame under the two heads "Hate, & sensual Folly"; but he sums it up so as to repudiate it, vehemently denying what his dreams have seemed to charge him with:

> Such Punishments, I thought, were due
> To Natures, deepliest stain'd with Sin,
> Still to be stirring up anew
> The self-created Hell within;
> The Horror of their Crimes to view,
> To know & loathe, yet wish & do!
> With such let Fiends make mockery—
> But I—O wherefore this on *me*?
> Frail is my Soul, yea, strengthless wholly,
> Unequal, restless, melancholy;
> But free from Hate, & sensual Folly!

---

*The *Notebooks* describe the contents of many dreams and nightmares in detail.

To live belov'd is all I need,
And whom I love, I love indeed.[84]

The frightful fiend is his own bad self, the angry and aggressive, concupiscent, self-seeking part he could not acknowledge.[85] And because he could not acknowledge it, because he continued to hold the fiend at arm's length in a lifelong paralysis of blind denial and dissociation instead of closing with it, Coleridge never changed. He was a remarkably unchanging man.

Coleridge made up his mind early in his life *to be innocent*. Writing at the age of twenty-four to his friend John Thelwall, a democrat, libertarian, and atheist, he admonishes him against speaking contemptuously of Christianity. Like Thelwall, he declares, he means to speak his mind freely on all subjects: "I will express *all* my feelings; but will previously take care to make my feelings benevolent. Contempt is Hatred without fear—Anger Hatred accompanied with apprehension. But because Hatred is always evil, Contempt must be always evil—& a good man ought to speak *contemptuously* of nothing." [86] He won't shrink from saying everything he feels, but he will take care "previously" to feel nothing but what is kind and generous! Such ingenuous disingenuousness had a personal source in Coleridge's terror of his own aggressive feelings; and a social source in the sentimentalized English puritanism of the eighteenth century. Coleridge needed to believe in his own benevolence. And he *was* benevolent, eagerly exerting himself for others. But his benevolence was not only the pure "disinterested Enthusiasm for others," the "eager Spirit of Self-sacrifice" [87] he maintained it was. There was self-interest in it too. Lacking confidence in the strength of his own purposes, he pursued them vicariously through others. Behind his self-abnegation lay a need to lean on others, cling to others. Vicariousness is an indirect form of self-interest, working for oneself by helping another's work; plagiarism is helping oneself to another's work. The one is often fine in

Coleridge, the other abject; but both sprang from a common root, his sense of his own weakness and dependency. He who knew how to distinguish so keenly could not distinguish between his dependency and his love.

Because Coleridge needed other people so, his eager helpfulness was often tainted with slavishness; he would suppress the anger and dislike he felt when his benevolence was repaid with something less. His swallowing his chagrin too much inevitably ended up in violent disappointment with other people's selfishness and ingratitude, the self-pitying conviction that his own unhappy fate was to love much but to be loved little in return. This was how he came to understand his friendship with Wordsworth. He gave his friend what few poets have ever received, the unstinting aid and encouragement of a fellow poet, powerful critic, and ebullient spirit, getting very little back from Wordsworth in the way of encouragement for his own work. He drew support from Wordsworth for himself, but he had to draw it. Wordsworth's cold, disliking note on *The Ancient Mariner* in the second edition of the *Lyrical Ballads* (he was afraid the poem's uncouthness had prejudiced readers against the volume) was shocking, not because Wordsworth felt that way but because he acted against his friend in publishing his feeling. But Coleridge would not admit to himself the anger he felt against Wordsworth in this case and in many others.

After their quarrel he spoke bitterly enough; the anger had been there all along and it lasted, through the patching up of things between them, till death. Writing to Thomas Allsop in December 1818, he said:

> I have loved with enthusiastic self-oblivion those who have been so well-pleased that I should, year after year, flow with a hundred nameless rills into *their* Main Stream, that they could find nothing but cold praise and effective discouragement of every attempt of mine to roll onward in a distinct current of my own—who *admitted* that the Ancient Mariner, the Christabel, the Re-

morse, and *some* pages of the Friend were not without merit, but were abundantly anxious to acquit their judgements of any blindness to the very numerous defects.[88]

There is an allusion in this sentence to Wordsworth's 1806 poem *A Complaint*, in which Wordsworth regrets the change in Coleridge following the latter's return from Malta and Italy a half-broken man:

> There is a change—and I am poor;
> Your love hath been, nor long ago,
> A Fountain at my fond Heart's door,
> Whose only business was to flow;
> And flow it did; nor taking heed
> Of its own bounty, or my need.

It is striking, in these fine lines, how freely Wordsworth acknowledges that Coleridge gave generously and he took needily. Coleridge may convict him of egotistical complacency, but not of blindness and self-deception about what had passed between them: he took, says Wordsworth, from Coleridge in his need, and he took again. Coleridge, however, blindly insisted that he never took anything for himself; he only gave disinterestedly, needing one thing only, "to be belov'd."

In the last few years of the friendship Coleridge began to mutter wretchedly in his notebooks against Wordsworth's egotism and against the worshipping and self-worshipping group formed by Dorothy, William, and Mary. An 1809 entry, masked in Greek letters, is a riddle (heavily inked out in the manuscript and not completely reconstructable) which sums up the tight little Wordsworth circle in the term *gynandrian incest*:

> Wife sister husband—husband sister wife
> Gynandrian incest's union, nature's strife.[89]

But Coleridge would not consider how much he himself contributed to the idolatrous atmosphere by having prostrated himself for so long before "his god Wordsworth" (the words are Charles Lamb's). The quarrel between the two, at the end of 1810, came right after his living for a while with the Wordsworths under one roof. The undomestic Coleridge, miserably unhappy at this time, was "an absolute nuisance in the family," so Wordsworth was supposed to have said about him— not to him. Its being repeated to Coleridge by a third person caused the quarrel. Wordsworth said other, harsher things as well, which in repetition became downright cruel. The Wordsworths had lost all hope for Coleridge, who seemed completely ruined by opium and gin and brandy. That good man Crabb Robinson labored to repair the breach. Coleridge wrote in 1813, "A Reconciliation has taken place—but the *Feeling*, which I had previous to that moment, when the 3/4ths Calumny burst like a Thunder-storm from a blue Sky on my Soul—after 15 years of such religious, almost superstitious, Idolatry & Self-sacrifice—O no! no! that I fear, never can return." [90] So Coleridge had known his adulation of Wordsworth was idolatrous (even as he harbored unexpressed resentments against him). He had made a kind of bargain: "religious" adulation of Wordsworth in return for, among other things, Wordsworth's forbearance and friendship. But the bargain couldn't stand up under the strain of living together in the same house.*

The nearest he comes to raising a question with himself about his own benevolence and self-sacrificing spirit follows a comment on Wordsworth's selfish complacency (as he deemed it) in his marriage:

> A blessed Marriage for him & for her it has been! But O! wedded Happiness is the intensest sort of Prosperity, & all Prosperity, I find, hardens the Heart—and happy people become so *very pru-*

---

*The comment of Mrs. Coleridge, whom the Wordsworth people treated with condescension, was, "His dearest & most indulgent friends . . . when he comes to live *wholly* with them, are *as* clear-sighted to his failings, & much *less* delicate in speaking of them, than his Wife."—CL III, 437n.

dent & far-sighted—but they look forward so constantly as not to have ever glanced at the retrospect, at their own feelings, & the principles consequent on them, when they were themselves disquieted, & their physical & moral Instincts not gratified!—O human Nature!—I tremble, lest my own tenderness of Heart, my own disinterested Enthusiasm for others, and eager Spirit of Self-sacrifice, should be owing almost wholly to my being & having ever been, an unfortunate unhappy Man.[91]

In that last sentence is a recognition of the neediness that played a part in Coleridge's generous helpfulness.

The fiend that Coleridge struggled to hold at arm's length was compounded not only of his fear of his own anger and assertiveness, but also of his sensuality ("Hate, & sensual Folly!"). Here too he had made up his mind to be innocent. Love requires more than virtue; it requires innocence, he wrote in his notebook in 1805: "Würde, Worthiness, VIRTUE consists in the mastery over the sensuous & sensual impulses—but Love requires INNOCENCE / Let the Lover ask his Heart whether he can endure that his Mistress should have *struggled* with a sensual impulse for another man tho' she overcame it from a sense of Duty to him?"[92] Coleridge was always nervous about his sexual desires, in a quite ordinary way—though judging by the jeering poem, with all its innuendo, that he wrote at nineteen about the Reverend Smerdon and his wife, he seems to have been more lighthearted on the subject in his youth. He enjoyed a short period of married contentment in which his "physical & moral Instincts" found gratification; this was ended by the discord which grew up between himself and Mrs. Coleridge. After their separation he condemned the natural man in him to death by concentrating all his longing on Sara Hutchinson, whom he could not marry because his conscience would not allow him to be divorced. Sara Coleridge was a good-looking woman. Sara Hutchinson was as plain as her sister Mary, Wordsworth's wife. In fixing his affection on Wordsworth's sister-in-law, Coleridge followed Wordsworth in a kind of renunciation of sensual ambition. But Coleridge, going beyond Wordsworth, renounced the marriage bed entirely. He knew what he was doing. Sara Hutchinson was an "Ideal Object" to him rather than a real one, a "yearning Thought that liv[ed] but in the brain" rather than a "living Love"—so he describes her in *Constancy to an Ideal Object*. She was the idea of love, not a woman whom he would or could love in marriage; addressing that "Ideal Object," that "yearning Thought," he writes, "She is not thou, and only thou art she."

As part of his renunciation of sexual life, Coleridge struggled continually to make his mind "pure," to train himself into innocence. He was always feverishly apprehensive lest in his dreams and daydreams he should stain his love for Sara Hutchinson by allowing desire to insinuate itself into his thought of her. While living abroad, his notebooks tell us, he dreamt

> a long Dream, of my Return, Welcome, &c, full of *Joy & Love*, wholly without *desire*, or bodily Inquietude, tho' with a most curious detail of images, and imagined actions, that might be supposed absolutely to *imply* awakened Appetite. A Proof this of the little Power Images have over Feelings or Sensation, Independent of the Will—compared with the power of Feelings over Images:— a proof too, one of a thousand, that by rigorous unremitting Purity of our Thought, when awake, joined with the unremitting Feeling of intense *Love*, the imagination in Sleep may become almost incapable of combining base or low Feelings with the Object of that Love.

Fear of his own sensuality leads him into disingenuous psychologizing about images, feelings, and the will. The failure of highly suggestive images to waken desire in him seems proof, not that his "Purity of Thought" and will has defeated his lust, but only that it has caused his lust to wear a mask of indifference when it shows itself in his dream. Coleridge did not kill the natural man in himself only by neglect, by becoming too much abstracted in his thoughts; he also killed him by disavowing and disassociating some of his strongest feelings.

His further comment on the dream shows how much it was concerned with the *wish* for innocence, for escape from his own sensuality: "In the Dream I supposed myself in a state of Society, like that of those great Priests of Nature who formed the Indian Worship in its purity, when all things, strictly of Nature, were reverenced according to their importance, undebauched by associations of Shame and Impudence, the twin-children of sensuality."[93] He longs for the state of nature, for the state of ignorant simplicity, for relief from the shame his own desires cause him ("Desire with Loathing strangely mixt")—that shame, he says, which is the child of sensuality. He longs for the stopped springs of his life to flow freely. But shame is not the child of sensuality. It is rather the other way around: sensuality is the child of shame. After Adam and Eve feel the shame of their nakedness they know the delight of their nakedness, which is sensuality. Shame is the fruit of the Tree of the Knowledge of Good and Evil, and sensuality is the fruit of shame. Or to put it straightforwardly: Sensuality is self-conscious sexual pleasure; it belongs to that self-consciousness which Coleridge otherwise exalted as the height of the human. Afraid to know his own concupiscent and aggressive nature, he clung to the delusion of his innocence. His fears and his delusions were mocked in his dreams by a whorish figure with red lips, free looks, yellow locks, and a leprous-white skin, a figure mixing Desire and Loathing. In the first version of *The Ancient Mariner* she was described as being "far liker Death" than Death, but she had no name. By the time Coleridge made his final revision, the best of his life behind him, he knew her name:

> Her lips were red, her looks were free,
> Her locks were yellow as gold:
> Her skin was as white as leprosy,

> The Night-mare LIFE-IN-DEATH was she,
> Who thicks man's blood with cold.

In her the opposed forces of Desire and Loathing were so strangely mixed as to bring his affective life to a Hamlet standstill. Her figure luridly proclaims that his Hamletism involved more concrete and violent elements than his calmly abstract formula, "prevalence of the abstracting and generalizing habit over the practical," would ever suggest.

Coleridge's cherished maxim "Know thyself!" was not, in spite of the origin of the phrase, classical-Socratic: adherence to it promised "painful Self-Enquiry" (as his July 29, 1802, letter to Southey says) not tranquil wisdom, inner struggle not equanimity. And though he wished to be a Christian, his soul was no longer the living one of vigorous faith but a problematic self groaning under the burden of its divisions and appalled to feel its own existence becoming more and more spectral. As he wrote in *The Wanderings of Cain*, "The Lord is God of the Living only, the dead have another God." An early one of these modern dead, Coleridge longed for that unity of being in which "the head will not be disjoined from the heart, nor will speculative truth be alienated from practical wisdom. And vainly without the union of both shall we expect an opening of the inward eye to the glorious vision" of that God of the living whose "existence admits of no question out of itself, acknowledges no predicate but the I AM IN THAT I AM!" [94]

In the letter to Southey, Coleridge had told his brother-in-law that his self-knowledge was "frustrated by the small pain" it gave him—he didn't feel it, there was something anaesthetic and dead about it. This is contradicted by his notebooks, which regularly record passages of self-judgment expressing the utmost pain. But of course such painful self-seeing was not a steady, relentless contemplation (who could bear it?); it was an intermittent sciatical nerve-flash, preceded and suc-

ceeded by an habitual state that Coleridge describes as a kind
of nervous limbo:

> 'Tis a strange place, this Limbo!—not a Place,
> Yet name it so:—Where Time and weary Space
> Fettered from flight, with night-mare sense of fleeing,
> Strive for their last crepuscular half-being.

His attentive looking inward led to "practical" inertness, a
condition of "crepuscular half-being," not to "that action"
which, he says in his 1812 lecture on *Hamlet*, "is the chief end
of existence."* Just here, however, lay the *greatest* pain, the
mystery, the despair—the despair of failing to exist at all. The
confident "I am" of self-assured, self-evident life has turned
into the guilty "am I?" of death-in-life. In the very late poem
Phantom or Fact, whose mournful visionary lucidity is punctu-
ated, not spoiled, by the clumsy interlocutory of the Friend,
he describes how in a dream his own spirit, himself as he was
meant to be, descended to him from heaven and sat beside
his bed.

AUTHOR

> A lovely form there sate beside my bed,
> And such a feeding calm† its presence shed,
> A tender love so pure from earthly leaven,
> That I unnethe the fancy might control,
> 'Twas my own spirit newly come from heaven,
> Wooing its gentle way into my soul!
> But ah! the change—It had not stirr'd, and yet—

---

*Sometimes Coleridge, in rebellion against his own moral-existential judg-
ment and self-judgment, indulges in a fit of mad romantic ideality—as when
he suggests in a notebook entry that any concrete act of realization, even the
realization of the Divine Idea in the Creation, is a fall into limitation and
"meanness": "Something inherently mean in action. Even the Creation of the
Universe disturbs my Idea of the Almighty's greatness—would do so, but that
I conceive that Thought with him Creates."—N 1. 1072. This is an ultimate
self-justification!

†See Wordsworth's *Prelude* IV, 279 ("feeding pleasures") for the source of this
lovely phrase. See also XIV (1850), 193 ("feeding source").

Alas! that change how fain would I forget!
That shrinking back, like one that had mistook!
That weary, wandering, disavowing look!
'Twas all another, feature, look and frame,
And still, methought, I knew, it was the same!

FRIEND

This riddling tale, to what does it belong?
Is't history? vision? or an idle song?
Or rather say at once, within what space
Of time this wild disastrous change took place?

AUTHOR

Call it a moment's work (and such it seems)
This tale's a fragment from the life of dreams;
But say, that years matur'd the silent strife,
And 'tis a record from the dream of life.

The silent strife between Coleridge's true self and his actual self, a strife that matured over the years, is summed up in the moment's work of a dream; a luminous moment from the life of his dreams terribly expresses the empty dream of his life.

"Coleridge is the intellectual centre of the English Romantic Movement," René Wellek writes in *Kant in England*.

> Without him, we should feel that English Romanticism—glorious as its poetry and prose [are] in [their] artistic achievements—remained dumb in matters of the intellect. We can extract a point of view, a certain attitude from the writings of Shelley and Keats, we find the expression of a creed in Wordsworth, but only in Coleridge we leave thought which is an integral part of poetry for thought which can be expressed in logical form and can claim comparison with the systems of the great German philosophers of the time.[95]

How flattered Coleridge would have been by Professor Wellek's judgment! He who felt he had achieved so little, always getting ready to write his philosophical Great Work (*magnum opus*), but only getting ready, might claim comparison with the great

German philosophers of his time. Yet he would not have been flattered to the top of his bent. Greater than the philosopher was the poet-philosopher, a summit he might look at from below but never really hoped to climb himself (pinning his hopes instead on Wordsworth). "[Humphrey] Davy in the kindness of his heart calls me the Poet-philosopher," he wrote to Thomas Poole in 1801; Davy, however was being kind; "I hope, Philosophy & poetry will not neutralize each other, & leave me an inert mass."[96] The poet-philosopher was greater than the philosopher because poetry was greater than philosophy—"For poetry is the blossom and the fragrancy of all human knowledge, human thoughts, human passions, emotions, language,"[97] and therefore *"the Poet* is the Greatest possible character!"[98] All great poetry was philosophical, all great poets were philosophers:

> A great Poet must be, implicitè if not explicitè, a profound Metaphysician. He may not have it in logical coherence, in his Brain & Tongue; but he must have it by *Tact* / for all sounds, & forms of human nature he must have the *ear* of a wild Arab listening in the silent Desart, the eye of a North American Indian tracing the footsteps of an Enemy upon the Leaves that strew the Forest—; the *Touch* of a Blind Man feeling the face of a darling Child.[99]

Shakespeare was a "profound philosopher": "In [his] *poems,* the creative power, and intellectual energy wrestle as in a war embrace. Each in its excess of strength seems to threaten the extinction of the other. At length in the DRAMA they were reconciled, and fought each with its shield before the breast of the other."[100]

But if all great poets were philosophers, by poet-philosopher Coleridge meant something more particular, something Lucretian yet going beyond Lucretius—for "Whatever in Lucretius is Poetry is not philosophical, whatever is philosophical is not Poetry."[101] In the poet-philosopher the logical, systematic thought Professor Wellek speaks about would have been "an integral part of the poetry," and the poetry would have realized itself in "logical form"—metaphor would have been married to method in a glorious "coadunation" of imagination and discursive reasoning. But Coleridge himself was only a poet *and* a philosopher, now the one (so very briefly) and now the other; till the poet committed suicide so as "not to think of what [he] needs must feel," of his life stripped of love and hope, the philosopher murdered the "natural man" by "abstruse research."

At the end of 1796, on the eve of making friends with Wordsworth and bursting forth with the not especially "thoughtful" *Ancient Mariner*, *Kubla Khan* and *Christabel*, he said about himself to John Thelwall, "I *think* too much for a *Poet*." His friend Southey, on the other hand, thought "too little for a *great* Poet." And it occurred to Coleridge "that an admirable Poet might be made by *amalgamating him & me*." [102] That impossible project was in fact undertaken, not with Southey but with Wordsworth. It was Coleridge's idea, which he proposed not long after the two men became friends in 1797, that Wordsworth should write a great philosophical poem, the wildly ambitious scheme of which Coleridge masterminded and pressed upon his not unwilling friend. Coleridge believed that "The Recluse," as the projected poem was called, would be the first truly philosophical poem ever written. Some six years after the two men first discussed the plan, the poem still remained to be written. Although Wordsworth immediately sat down to the job, nothing happened; he was struck dumb. The prolonged poetic self-examination this failure set off in him became *The Prelude*, worked up through the years through numerous stages. *The Prelude* consists of autobiographical recollections of the growth of Wordsworth's own sensibility into imagination and poetry*; it is not at all the excogitation in verse of a great philosophical system of the unity of "Man,

---

*Though *The Prelude* is an early work in the modern genre of art-about-art, it is not a Portrait of the Artist as a Young Man, because there is so little of the portrait about it. We get a detailed account of Wordsworth's states of mind and feeling, exultations and depressions, reflections and illuminations, but

Nature & Society." But Wordsworth didn't give up on "The Recluse." Though he stopped thinking of the poem about himself as forming a part of "The Recluse," the latter remained his central, his main goal, to which *The Prelude*, though it grew at last to fourteen books, was always subsidiary, something which prepared the way for the greater one to come. Nor did Coleridge give up either: in a letter written at the beginning of 1804 we find him continuing to "affirm" that Wordsworth

> will hereafter be admitted as the first & greatest philosophical Poet—the only man who has effected a compleat and constant synthesis of Thought & Feeling and combined them with Poetic Forms, with the music of pleasurable passion and with Imagination or the *modifying* Power in that highest sense of the word in which I have ventured to oppose it to Fancy, or the aggregating power—in that sense in which it is a dim Analogue of Creation, not all that we can *believe* but all that we can *conceive* of creation. Wordsworth is a Poet, and I feel myself a better Poet, in knowing how to honour *him*, than in all my own poetic Compositions, all I have done or hope to do—and I prophesy immortality to his *Recluse*, as the first & finest philosophical Poem, if only it be (as it undoubtedly will be) a Faithful Transcript of his own most august & innocent Life, of his own habitual Feelings & Modes of seeing and hearing.[103]

Very early in his life Wordsworth aspired to erect "a monument" of English verse. While still in his teens at Cambridge, *The Prelude* reports, he felt himself "a dedicated spirit" (IV, 344). In those days of "morning gladness" there came to him

> a daring thought, that I might leave
> Some monument behind me which pure hearts
> Should reverence. The instinctive humbleness,

---

we don't get Wordsworth himself. A *Spectator ab extra,* as Coleridge called him, Wordsworth contemplated not only the world but also himself from a distance, and that inner distance hides the man from us. The same is true of the work of another great memory writer—Proust's narrator Marcel unfolds an enormous wealth of observation and self-observation, but he doesn't unfold himself; he is a sensibility, not a person.

Upheld even by the very name and thought
Of printed books and authorship, began
To melt away.

(VI, 67)

Ambitious of the highest fame, he meant to carve a niche for
himself beside Spenser, Shakespeare, and Milton by writing a
great work, ideas for which he had been revolving in his head
ever since he first thought of himself as a poet. But till Wordsworth met Coleridge, "great work" meant to him what it
meant to everybody before the modern era, an heroic poem
(epic) or a tragedy. And since he knew he was no tragedian,
all his thoughts aimed at heroic subjects. Book I of *The Prelude*
tells how the young poet considered carrying out Milton's idea
of an epic on King Arthur ("some old Romantic tale by Milton
left unsung"); or following Spenser into "the groves of Chiv-
alry" and writing an epic romance about knightly feats and
dire enchantments; or treating the Virgilian theme of a van-
quished hero (Mithridates) who passes northward to father "a
race by whom Perished the Roman Empire"; or singing the
exploits of more modern heroes of truth and liberty. Toward
the end of his catalogue, however, he implies that such tradi-
tionally heroic themes, reverence them though he did, were
too remote from his "own passions and habitual thoughts,"
and he turns to two projects nearer his "own heart." These
are for a narrative poem—

Some tale from my own heart, more near akin
To my own passions and habitual thoughts,
Some variegated story, in the main
Lofty, with interchange of gentler things

—and for a "philosophical song," the idea of which had been
planted in him by Coleridge:

Then, last wish—
My last and favourite aspiration—then
I yearn towards some philosophic song

Of truth that cherishes our daily life,
With meditations passionate from deep
Recesses in man's heart, immortal verse
Thoughtfully fitted to the Orphean lyre;
But from this awful burthen I full soon
Take refuge, and beguile myself with trust
That mellower years will bring a riper mind
And clearer insight.

(I, 228)

So Wordsworth found the epic subjects grand but dead. On the other hand, the subjects which engaged his active thoughts and feelings were not epical, and to be a great poet you had to write an epic. His preferred subjects were indeed "lofty," yet implicated in "gentler things" and "daily life"; they were bound up with a quiet life which was at the opposite pole from the nobly, the martially heroic. The problem he was struggling with was how to be great. The way to greatness for poets of an earlier age had been along a clearly marked route; they only needed to follow it. But now every poet had to be "his own Aristotle," as Byron unsolemnly put it some years later. * No longer did you win the laurel by toeing a known mark and racing straight for the goal before you; you found your own way as you went along, unsure if it *was* the way.

Wordsworth counted on Coleridge to show him the way to greatness—that is, how to write a modern epic. *The Prelude* was not a Great Work, only a tryout for one, testing whether Wordsworth really did possess "the visionary

---

* If ever I should condescend to prose,
    I'll write poetical commandments, which
Shall supersede beyond all doubt all those
    That went before; in these I shall enrich
My text with many things that no one knows,
    And carry precept to the highest pitch:
I'll call my work "Longinus o'er a Bottle,
Or, Every Poet his *own* Aristotle."

(*Don Juan* I, CCIV)

power," whether there was in him "possible sublimity" (II, 337). *The Prelude* was only himself thinking about himself and his own mind—self not world, the self "moving about in worlds not realized," discovering the *power* of imagination to go out to nature and realize worlds (but not in fact realizing a world). An autobiographical poem could never be an epic— egotistical sublimity did not extend *that* far. *The Prelude* was long enough, God knows, but it did not encompass anything like that totality of life which is so essential to the epic story. It was not essential that the epic should be the "heroic trumpet" Wordsworth calls it at the end of *Home at Grasmere*, in bidding ambiguous farewell to the active, turbulent, combative side of his nature, to the "forwardness of Soul" which had led him in his youth to think of a soldier's career for himself and then of writing a soldierly poem. With Milton's example (as always) before him, it was no hard thing for Wordsworth to give up the idea of a martial poem. As Milton had written, there were arguments

> Not less but more Heroic than the wrath
> Of stern Achilles on his Foe pursued
> Thrice Fugitive about Troy Wall; or rage
> Of Turnus for Lavinia disespoused,
> Or Neptune's ire or Juno's, that so long
> Perplexed the Greek and Cytherea's Son.

(Par. Lost IX, 14)

The encompassing of all of human life was the chief feature of the philosophical poem Coleridge urged on Wordsworth. It was to be an epic poem in its scope, even though the projected epic had ceased to be a story of men warring and had become a poem of meditations and reflections. The question remained whether you could have an epic without men *acting*, but "The Recluse" was designed to answer that question.

Wordsworth's dependency on Coleridge for writing "The Recluse" was extreme. The general idea of the work had been a matter of conversation between them going back at least to

1798. But Wordsworth wanted Coleridge to supply him with detailed written notes as well. With *The Prelude* nearly completed by the spring of 1804, he began to think urgently about the "larger and more important work to which it is tributary"* and pressed his friend for help: "I am very anxious to have your notes for the Recluse," he wrote on March 6, 1804; "I cannot say how much importance I attach to this, if it should please God that I survive you, I should reproach myself for ever in writing the work if I had neglected to procure this help." When he heard from Coleridge three weeks later that Coleridge had been near death from illness, he exclaimed very unphlegmatically (March 29, 1804):

> Your last letter but one informing us of your late attack was the severest shock to me, I think, I have ever received. . . . I will not speak of other thoughts that passed through me; but I cannot help saying that I would gladly have given 3 fourths of my possessions for your letter on the Recluse at that time. I cannot say what a load it would be to me, should I survive you and you die without this memorial left behind. Do, for heaven's sake, put this out of reach of accident immediately.

The urgency of his letter is like that of a policeman imploring an expiring victim to say who his attacker was before he dies. "But although Coleridge did not die, no notes were ever forthcoming. Later he said that he had sent them from Malta, but the person who carried them, Major Adye, died on the way home of plague; all his luggage was burnt and the notes among it. Coleridge never rewrote them. . . . This was a fatal blow to William's hopes."[104] Instead of "The Recluse," Wordsworth wrote *The Excursion*, which was very different from the great work the two friends had once schemed about with so much excitement.

The heart of Coleridge's scheme for "The Recluse" was

*"This poem will not be published these many years, and never during my lifetime, till I have finished a larger and more important work to which it is tributary."—To Thomas De Quincey, March 6, 1804.

to achieve epic totality not in the old way—through some primary story, legendary or historical—but discursively, yet poetically, by means of *a system of philosophy*. We know this thanks to the letter Coleridge wrote to Wordsworth on May 30, 1815, in reply to Wordsworth's asking him for his criticisms of the recently published *Excursion*—a letter written long years after the morning days of their friendship and collaboration in 1797–98. Wordsworth had learned from a common friend that Coleridge had criticized that poem for treating commonplaces and truisms as if they were deep and weighty truths wrung by the poet from his own experiences, feelings, and reason. So they were to Wordsworth—hardwon convictions. But these, said Coleridge, "come almost as Truisms or common-place to others." [105] Defending his poem even as he solicited Coleridge's opinion of it, Wordsworth wrote in his letter of May 22, 1815, that one of his principal aims had "been to put the commonplace truths, of the human affections especially, in an interesting point of view; and rather to remind men of their knowledge, as it lurks inoperative and unvalued in their own minds, than to attempt to convey recondite or refined truths." Thus if he did not now, so many years later, quite disclaim all philosophical pretensions, he disclaimed any pretensions to philosophizing deeply "On Man, on Nature, and on Human Life," as he himself had put it in *Home at Grasmere* (754).* There, some fifteen years before, he had prayed the muse, in highest epic style, to help him "sing"

> Of Truth, of Grandeur, Beauty, Love and Hope,
> And melancholy Fear subdued by Faith;
> Of blessed consolations in distress;
> Of moral strength, and intellectual Power;
> Of joy in widest commonalty spread;

*In his preface to *The Excursion* Wordsworth quoted the concluding lines of the unpublished *Home at Grasmere* as a "Prospectus" of what his ambition aimed at (or one should say *had* aimed at) in "The Recluse."

Of the individual Mind that keeps her own
Inviolate retirement, subject there
To Conscience only, and the law supreme
Of that Intelligence which governs all.

(767)

But now he consented only to be the philosopher of homely truths that everybody knew but did not heed.

Coleridge, in his long reply of May 30, 1815, supposed the homely truths had been the concern of Wordsworth's occasional verse, and he reminded Wordsworth that they had planned "The Recluse" to be

> a *Philosophical Poem*, the result and fruits of a Spirit so fram'd & so disciplin'd, as had been told in the [*Prelude*]. Whatever in Lucretius is Poetry is not philosophical, whatever is philosophical is not Poetry: and in the very Pride of confident Hope I looked forward to the Recluse, as the *first* and *only* true Phil. Poem in existence. Of course, I expected the Colors, Music, imaginative Life, and Passion of *Poetry*; but the matter and arrangement of *Philosophy*—not doubting from the advantages of the Subject that the Totality of a System was not only capable of being harmonized with, but even calculated to aid, the unity (Beginning, Middle and End) of a *Poem*.

Coleridge had expected a poem which would be a poem in all respects, but one which would have the matter and arrangement of philosophy and an embracing unity deriving from the totality of the philosophical system the poem would set forth. Coleridge then outlined the philosophical epic they had projected as follows:

> I supposed you first to have meditated the faculties of Man in the abstract, in their correspondence with his Sphere of action, and first, in the Feeling, Touch, and Taste, then in the Eye, & last in the Ear, to have laid a solid and immoveable foundation for the Edifice by removing the sandy Sophisms of Locke, and the Mechanic Dogmatists, and demonstrating that the Senses were living growths and developements of the Mind & Spirit in a much

juster as well as higher sense, than the mind can be said to
be formed by the Senses—. Next, I understood that you would
take the Human Race in the concrete . . .—to have affirmed a
Fall in some sense, as a fact, the possibility of which cannot be
understood from the nature of the Will, but the reality of which
is attested by Experience & Conscience—Fallen men contemplated in the different ages of the World, and in the different
states—Savage—Barbarous—Civilized—the lonely Cot, or Bor-
derer's Wigwam—the Village—the Manufacturing Town—Sea-
port—City—Universities—and not disguising the sore evils,
under which the whole Creation groans, to point out however a
manifest Scheme of Redemption from this Slavery, of Reconciliation from this Enmity with Nature—what are the Obstacles, the
Antichrist that must be & already is—and to conclude by a grand
didactic swell on the necessary identity of a true Philosophy
with true Religion, agreeing in the results and differing only as
the analytic and synthetic process, as discursive from intuitive,
the former chiefly useful as perfecting the latter—in short, the
necessity of a general revolution in the modes of developing &
disciplining the human mind by the substitution of Life, and
Intelligence . . . for the philosophy of mechanism which in
everything that is most worthy of the human Intellect strikes
Death. . . . In short, Facts elevated into Theory—Theory into
Laws—and laws into living and intelligent Powers—true Idealism necessarily perfecting itself in Realism, & Realism refining
itself into Idealism.—

Such or something like this was the Plan, I had supposed that
you were engaged on.[106]

The scheme of "The Recluse" as he describes it here is char-
acteristically Coleridgian in its world-devouring ambition.
There is also an obvious Coleridgian, un-Wordsworthian slant
to the ideas—in the emphasis on the priority of mind, in the
affirmation of a Fall, and in the forced identification of the
"Reconciliation from this Enmity with Nature" with Christian
redemption. One can be sure that the poet who asked (in
Home at Grasmere) why Paradise and Elysian groves and Fortunate Fields should not be "a simple produce of the common

day," rather than things that had never been or had been long ago, never engaged himself to write an Anglican epic. But some kind of grand epic work, a Wordsworthian epic of man meditating on the largest scale, he passionately longed to write. So he had eagerly accepted his friend's encouragement and help and had been drawn into what he usually kept clear of, a Coleridge project whose pretensions alone guaranteed its failure. For in this one matter Coleridge's impotent grandiosity and Wordsworth's baffled epic ambitions coincided. Wordsworth failed to write "The Recluse" not because he could not put his heart and genius into what was really a Coleridge project, nor because his ailing and unhappy friend could no longer flow for him with his old bounty, but because "The Recluse" was impossible to write—the road to modern epicality did not lie that way. Indeed, it did not lie with poetry at all, which was fast losing the power to tell any kind of story, epic or otherwise, but with the novel. Modern epicality, such as it is, as ambiguous as it is, belongs to the novel.

What Coleridge offered Wordsworth in the plan of "The Recluse" was a chance to write a modern thinking epic, thanks to which Wordsworth might stand beside or even above Milton. What did "The Recluse" offer Coleridge? What was in it for him? He looked to Wordsworth to show the way to that "compleat and constant synthesis of Thought & Feeling," speculation and action, mind and nature, which was the goal of his own philosophical efforts, and the want of which in his life was his Hamlet tragedy. Because he thought too much for a poet, he could not be the poet-philosopher except through the poet Wordsworth, whom he would furnish with the necessary philosophical know-how; and through Coleridge, Wordsworth would fulfill the highest task of the modern poet by writing "the *first* and *only* true Phil. Poem in existence." Coleridge's obstructed spirit longed to flow into that of his friend's: "O that my Spirit purged by Death of its Weaknesses, which are alas! my *identity*, might flow into *thine*, & live and act in thee, & be Thou," he wrote in his notebook in Sicily in 1805.[107]

Yet Coleridge was no more able, as a philosopher, to supply Wordsworth with a system than he was able, as a poet, to write the epic himself. He might provide Wordsworth with philosophical inspiration, ideas, arguments. But a philosophical *system*? A complete *system* of the unity of mind and nature, elaborated in its essentials and set forth in some kind of order, was exactly what he was never able to work out in his whole lifetime, as he was never able to work out anything systematically. His reliance was ultimately on his stronger friend, who was here relying on him. But of course it was a hopeless, wrong idea all along to think of *"amalgamating him & me."*

With Romanticism the imagination, in a kind of second Fall, became self-conscious and knew itself. It knew itself as a double thing: as a natural, spontaneous, uncalculating, and unselfconscious activity on the one hand; and as a purposeful, highly calculating, and self-conscious—"unnatural"— activity on the other. This doubleness is evident in Coleridge's view that Shakespeare's judgment is equal to his genius. It is of course evident in his calling art "the mediatress between, and reconciler of, nature and man." [108] It is also evident in his distinction between a primary and a secondary imagination. The primary (or common) imagination is "the living Power . . . of all human Perception" and is largely unconscious. The secondary (or poetic or uncommon) imagination is "an echo" of the primary, yet it "co-exist[s] with the conscious will. . . . It dissolves, diffuses, dissipates, in order to re-create; . . . it struggles to idealize and unify. It is essentially *vital*." [109] That is, the secondary imagination's activity is also unconscious, but "co-existing" with conscious, purposeful effort.

Coleridge calls both kinds of imagination "vital." Yet a certain suspicion attaches to the artistic (secondary) imagination because of its involvement with the conscious will. To the degree that art (self-conscious mind) enters into art, to the degree that the poet *struggles to idealize and unify*—sweats like

Yeats's scrubwoman on her marrow-bones instead of warbling wood-notes with effortless spontaneity—to the degree that art forces nature to be what it is not: to that degree the question arises whether art after all stands on the side of life, whether the modern poetic imagination is "essentially *vital*." For German Romanticism there was no question: art stood on the side of the mind, not of life, yearning across the gulf of self-consciousness for the nature from which it was cut off. The ancient Greeks, wrote Schiller in 1795 in his great essay "On Naive and Sentimental Poetry," living in the springtime of human history, "felt naturally; we are full of feeling *for* the natural. The emotion which animated the soul of Homer when he had his godly swineherd hospitably succor Ulysses was unquestionably a different one entirely from that which filled young Werther's breast when, coming home from a boring party, he read the story in Homer's poem. Our feeling for nature is like a sick man's for health." Almost a century and a half after Schiller wrote his essay, Thomas Mann said:

> It is romantic, when one sees in art not nature . . . but the reverse. In the duality of spirit and nature, whose fusion in the third kingdom hovers before the eyes of all romanticism as the goal of human nature, art is entirely relegated to the sphere of mind, being essentially and indubitably sense, consciousness, unity, purpose. Such was Novalis' meaning, when he called *Wilhelm Meister* "entirely a product of art, a work of understanding," and romanticists have never otherwise conceived art than as the opposite pole of the instinctive, natural and unconscious.[110]

For English Romanticism, however, the matter was more ambiguous; the poet felt less desperately situated. Modern self-consciousness of course weighed on the English poets too. But *through* poetry the English poet hoped to recover his life in nature; there he might hope to speak again, as Keats said, with "the true voice of feeling," the voice of Shakespeare and the elder poets. Keats opposed truth of feeling (nature) in poetry to the "false beauty proceeding from art"—meaning by *art* the highly self-conscious art of the preceding age. He had no tendency to think of the artistic mind per se as having become a cold intensity of self-conscious reflection, withering up all the natural man. So far indeed was Keats from feeling mind as an oppression that he reproached himself for being ignorant; he studied to know more; he read philosophy, so as to acquire something of that knowledge Coleridge liked to think had been the death of himself as a poet. To Coleridge, his own intellectuality was not only an oppression, it was a disease—he called it, as we have seen, "the *thinking* disease . . . in which feelings instead of embodying themselves in *acts* ascend, & become materials of general reasoning." Yet Coleridge's literary philosophy shows no inclination to minimize the role of thought in poetry. On the contrary! In Chapter 1 of the *Biographia* he tells us how he learned from his schoolmaster at Christ's Hospital that "poetry, even that of the loftiest and, seemingly, that of the wildest odes, had a logic of its own, as severe as that of science." [111] In Chapter 14 "the greatest lord of black magic in English lyrical poetry, the most incorrigible dreamer in the records of English biography" (as the editor of his Shakespearean criticism calls him), announces in capital letters, by way of an oracular wind-up to his definition of the poet, that "GOOD SENSE is the BODY of poetic genius"!*

The essence of Coleridge's preceding definition of the poet lies in the function he attributes to the poetic imagination of mediating between life and thinking-about-life.

> This power, first put in action by the will and understanding, and retained under their irremissive, though gentle and unnoticed, controul (*laxis effertur habenis* ['driven on with loose reins']) reveals itself in the balance or reconciliation . . . of the general, with the concrete; the idea, with the image; the individ-

---

*". . . FANCY [being] its DRAPERY, MOTION its LIFE, and IMAGINATION the SOUL that is everywhere, and in each; and forms all into one graceful and intelligent whole."—BL II, 16. Wordsworth also praised good sense, as the "one property of all poetry," in the Preface to the *Lyrical Ballads*.

ual, with the representative; . . . a more than usual state of emotion, with more than usual order; judgement ever awake and
steady self-possession, with enthusiasm and feeling profound or
vehement; and while it blends and harmonizes the natural and
the artificial,

life and the mind's effort to grasp life through the understanding—while it does all this, *nevertheless*, in the end, imagination "*still subordinates art to nature.*" [112] The art which embraces
nature in its order is overarched by nature's order. "The art itself is nature," as Coleridge, quoting from *The Winter's Tale,**
says subsequently about the union of "*spontaneous* impulse
and of *voluntary* purpose" in metrical language. [113]

Although the imagination is first put into action by the will
and understanding, for both the early and the late Coleridge
the writing of a poem was essentially a spontaneous, natural
motion of the living man; only secondarily was it a laborious
effort of consideration by the thinking man. A poem was the
poet's living *act*. Hamlet was no poet! Or rather Hamlet was
a poet just like Coleridge, a poet who was unable to write
poems. Poetry stood on the side of nature, a golden nature in
which the poet, dieted on paradisal milk and honey-dew, self-
consciousness cast off, loudly sounded his music in an Or-
phic ecstasy of flashing eyes and floating hair. Not to write
poems, for Coleridge, was not to "sing," and made part of
that death-in-life in which he also did not pair in love or build
a nest, only read and thought. All Nature seemed at work on
February 21, 1825, the slugs crawling, the bees stirring, the

---

*   nature is made better by no mean
    But nature makes that mean. So, over that art
    Which . . . adds to nature, is an art
    That nature makes. You see, sweet maid, we marry
    A gentler scion to the wildest stock,
    And make conceive a bark of baser kind
    By bud of nobler race. This is an art
    Which does mend nature—change it rather—but
    The art itself is nature.

                                                        (IV.iv.89)

birds on the wing—still sleeping Winter wore "on his smiling face a dream of Spring!" But Coleridge meanwhile, with his unsmiling lips and his head uncrowned with laurel, is

> the sole unbusy thing,
> Nor honey make[s], nor pair[s], nor build[s], nor sing[s].

For Wordsworth too, of course, poetry was a part of nature and belonged with honey-making, pairing in marriage, building a nest-home; for him, too, it was "singing." In Book V of *The Prelude*, which is entitled "Books," he proclaims "the great Nature that exists in works / Of mighty Poets" (V, 618). Yet Wordsworth's poetry of nature has a countercurrent which threatens to carry him *out* of nature—out of the common life of men and women, which he said "consumed the diviner spirit,"* into a desertlike, inhuman spiritual world a lot like Coleridge's nonpoetic desert of "the abstracting and generalizing" mind.†

---

*"Above all, have not the common duties and cares of common life, at all times exposed men to injury, from causes whose action is the more fatal from being silent and unremitting, and which, wherever it was not jealously watched and steadily opposed, must have pressed upon and consumed the diviner spirit."—"Answer to Mathetes," a contribution to Coleridge's *Friend* (I, 390). Long before, in *Tintern Abbey*, Wordsworth had exclaimed against the "dreary intercourse of daily life." He writes in *The Prelude* about
> these times of fear,
> This melancholy waste of hopes o'erthrown,
> . . . indifference and apathy
> And wicked exultation, when good men
> On every side fall off we know not how
> To selfishness, disguised in gentle names
> Of peace and quiet and domestic love—
> Yet mingled, not unwillingly, with sneers
> On visionary minds.

(II, 448)

---

†This super-natural Wordsworth, in whom "the light of sense goes out" to reveal "the invisible world," is A. C. Bradley's sublime and paradoxical, mystical and visionary Wordsworth, Geoffrey Hartman's apocalyptist who nervously backs off from apocalypse.

In that same Book V Wordsworth recounts a dream* which, as De Quincey wrote in his *Recollections of the Lake Poets,* "reaches the very *ne plus ultra* of sublimity." The landscape of this epic dream is the Hamlet desert of death-in-life, the "wild wilderness" of an "Arabian waste"; across the desert sand hurries a Bedouin mounted on a dromedary, who is at the same time the madman Don Quixote, in anxious flight before "the fleet waters of a drowning world." The Arab's "errand" is to save from the oncoming flood the stone of geometry, which he carries under one arm, and the shell of poetry, which he clutches in the opposite hand, while also bearing a martial lance before him. (He has his hands full!) Wordsworth says that he often liked to imagine this "phantom from the world of sleep, this semi-Quixote," as

> a living man—
> A gentle dweller in the desart, crazed
> By love, and feeling, and internal thought
> Protracted among endless solitudes—
> Have shaped him, in the oppression of his brain,
> Wandering upon this quest.
>
> (V, 143)

He did not, the poet tells us, pity this crazy knight of poetry and intellect, this lone bachelor of the desert, houseless yet with his hands as full as any householder's; no, he rather "reverenced" him. And then Wordsworth the cottager, the silent breather-in of domestic quiet and respecter of domestic duties, who asked rhetorically in later life if the skylark despised the earth where cares abound, or if he rather, even as he aspired with his wings toward heaven, still kept an eye

---

*Not one actually dreamt by Wordsworth, it seems, but a literary dream elaborated from a dream of Descartes'. In the earlier drafts of *The Prelude* the dream is given to "a friend"; in a late revision Wordsworth claims it for himself.

on his nest on the dewy ground; the Wordsworth who moralized the lark as the

> Type of the wise who soar, but never roam;
> True to the kindred points of Heaven and Home!
>
> (*To a Skylark*)

—that Wordsworth bursts out almost venomously against the home-dwellers, the comfortable lovers of their sweethearts, wives, and children, the homely livers of the common life whom he otherwise (he above all) esteemed as the essential human substance:

> Enow there are on earth to take in charge
> Their wives, their children, and their virgin loves,
> Or whatsoever else the heart holds dear—
> Enow to think of these—yea, will I say
>
> . . . .
>   that I methinks
> Could share that maniac's anxiousness, could go
> Upon like errand. Oftentimes at least
> Me hath such deep entrancement half-possessed
> When I have held a volume in my hand—
> Poor earthly casket of immortal verse—
> Shakespeare or Milton, labourers divine.
>
> (V, 153)

Wordsworth recounts the dream of the shell and the stone by way of introduction to the subject of books and their part, along with nature, in shaping his mind and imagination. His first thought about books, as a born British materialist, is that they are so frail, so perishable. Man's tutor nature is a material power as well as a noumenal one, a "bodily image" through which "the sovereign Intellect . . . hath diffused / A soul divine which we participate, / A deathless spirit"; as a massive material body it is the substantial and enduring earthly reality, not to perish till the end of days. But man's co-tutor, books, though also filled with "Things worthy of unconquerable life," must, Wordsworth can't help feeling, inevitably founder in the vicissitudes of earthly existence, by earthquake or fire or flood:

> Thou also, man, hast wrought,
> For commerce of thy nature with itself,
> Things worthy of unconquerable life;
> And yet we feel—we cannot chuse but feel—
> That these must perish.

Wordsworth goes on to say that the heart trembles at the thought that we shall no longer need all those "worthy things" wrought by the human spirit when we pass over into immortal being; but meanwhile man is a child of earth and all his works are vulnerable. Nature's "living Presence" would "still subsist Victorious" after an elemental catastrophe, but

> all the meditations of mankind,
> Yea, all the adamantine holds of truth
> By reason built, or passion (which itself
> Is highest reason in a soul sublime),
> The consecrated works of bard and sage,
> Sensuous or intellectual,

would be quite defeated and wiped out. Oh, why isn't there in nature something nearer to the human mind, by which it might participate in what Whitehead calls nature's "enormous permanences":

> Oh, why hath not the mind
> Some element to stamp her image on
> In nature somewhat nearer to her own?
> Why, gifted with such powers to send abroad
> Her spirit, must it lodge in shrines so frail?

(V, 17)

Wordsworth's anxiety about the survival of the works of poetry and intellect is striking, and strikingly apocalyptic—the dream perfectly expresses that feeling. The catastrophes he mentions are all natural ones. But it may be that his fears for man's spiritual culture derive most immediately from a biblical sense in him of the French Revolution as a great cleansing flood indiscriminately sweeping away an unjust old world and everything in it, whether deserving of destruction or not.

> I saw
> A glittering light, and asked [the Arab] whence it came.
> "It is," said he, "the waters of the deep
> Gathering upon us."
>
> (V, 128)

Wordsworth's sense of poetry here is that of a frail, delicate existence. Because poetry lacks nature's material robustness—because human spirituality is a delicate growth—poetry is menaced with destruction by overwhelming forces of earth.

But at the same time Wordsworth feels that poetry is strong, stronger than nature. In a great dithyramb near the end of Book V, he celebrates the imaginative power of childhood, rising responsively to meet the imaginative power of poets and storytellers: "Our childhood sits . . . upon a throne / That hath more power than all the elements"; and while we sit upon the throne of childhood, before we are unseated and bowed down by time and custom, before "we learn to live / In reconcilement with our stinted powers,"

> oh, then we feel, we feel,
> We know, when we have friends. Ye dreamers, then,
> Forgers of lawless tales, we bless you then—
> Imposters, drivellers, dotards, as the ape
> Philosophy will call you—then we feel
> With what, and how great might ye are in league,
> Who make our wish our power, our thought a deed,
> An empire, a possession. Ye whom time
> And seasons serve—all faculties—to whom
> Earth crouches, th' elements are potter's clay,

Space like a heaven filled up with northern lights,
Here, nowhere, there, and everywhere at once.

(V, 546)

Earth *crouches* before the imagination. Here poetry, just because it has so slight a foundation in material nature, is all-powerful. From this angle, there is nothing redemptive about the flood in the dream; it is purely destructive of man's creative mind. Now the dream is not looking backward to the biblical flood, but forward to what Yeats calls, so violently, "this filthy modern tide / And . . . its formless spawning fury" (*The Statues*) rising up to drown the world. Now it is poetry, defending the invisible things of the spirit, that will ultimately prove "victorious," not nature. Ghostly poetry, hailing the superhuman with "A mouth that has no moisture and no breath," takes arms against the sea of nature and by opposing "The fury and mire of human veins" overmasters it. In Yeats the smithies of art "break" the flood of nature:

> Astraddle on the dolphin's mire and blood,
> Spirit after spirit! The smithies break the flood,
> The golden smithies of the Emperor!
> Marbles of the dancing floor
> Break bitter furies of complexity,
> Those images that yet
> Fresh images beget,
> That dolphin-torn, that gong-tormented sea.

In Wordsworth's dream such a victory isn't looking likely yet; spirit is still very much on the run. Yet the gaunt, desert-dwelling Quixote* clutching shell and stone and being chased

---

*"The next day Wordsworth arrived from Bristol at Coleridge's cottage. I think I see him now. He answered in some degree to his friend's description of him, but was more gaunt and don Quixote-like. . . . There was a severe, worn pressure of thought about his temples, a fire in his eye, as if he saw something in objects more than the outward appearance. . . ."—Hazlitt, "My First Acquaintance with Poets."

by the flood is more than a madman ("in the blind and awful lair / Of such a madness, reason did lie couched" [V, 151]), more than a refugee; he is a soldier armed with a lance—surely he will turn and fight. Wordsworth's temper, if it was nothing else, was militant.

The Hamlet idea was no mere notion expounded by Coleridge in his lectures, it was his life, his fate—the fate of a soul cast out of life onto the wide wide sea of itself:

> Alone, alone, all, all alone,
> Alone on a wide wide sea!
> And Christ would take no pity on
> My soul in agony.[114]

He is among the first of that modern Hamlet company of delvers into their own inwardness, anguished or implacable meditators rather than soldierly performers, who strove, said Coleridge, as heroically as any soldier to "sound the depths of our being." In making notes for a lecture on "the original unific Consciousness, the primary Perception, & its extreme difficulty," he reminded himself

> to take occasion to draw a lively picture of the energies, self-denials, sacrifices, toils, trembling knees, & sweat-drops on the Brow, of a philosopher who has really been sounding the depths of our being—& to compare it with the greatest & most perseverant Labors of Travellers, Soldiers, and whomever else Men honor & admire—how trifling the latter! And yet how cold our gratitude to the former.[115]

Yeats justified himself in much the same way when he wrote: "Why should we honor those who die on the field of battle? A man may show as reckless a courage in entering into the abyss of himself."

Coleridge's justification of himself, with its stress upon the exertions, self-denials, and persevering hard work demanded by the Hamlet vocation, is made before the English middle-class conscience. He was not a feckless dreamer after all, he is saying. Yeats's justification of *his* Hamletism looks to a gentlemanly ideal and is full of swagger; he talks extravagantly about "reckless courage." Each, however, claims the honors of a soldier, thinks himself entitled to have

> for his passage
> The soldiers' music and the rites of war
>
> (V.ii.387)

allowed the dead Hamlet. But the abyss of the self is *not* the field of battle. Coleridge's life was *not* one of toiling self-denial, though it was certainly full of straining effort; though Yeats had a poet's courage, it was not a reckless trooper's courage. Each man defends himself as a spiritual soldier. But it is of the essence of the Hamlet career that one is *unable* to be a soldier, that one is *unable* to act in the world, and that therefore one has a smack of ignominiousness—moral courage and life-courage, sundered as they are by the division of the self, not being the same thing. Fortinbras says that Hamlet

> was likely, had he been put on,
> To have proved most royal.
>
> (V.ii.386)

But he wasn't put on, he didn't prove most royal.

Coleridge's strength, the strength of a man whom all, including himself, united in calling weak, gave out toward the end of his life. The Hamlet fate (to quote from Yeats's *Statues* again) is to grow "thin from eating flies," to learn at last that "knowledge increases unreality." Cursing his fate, cursing that self-knowledge commanded from the Greek heavens, Coleridge cried out, in a poem written two years before his death, *"Ignore thyself!"* But the laboring, stertorous, thick-syllabled, mind-ridden lines, which were the style of his late verse—a species of what Hermann Broch called "the style of

old age, the style of the essential, the style of the abstract"[116]
—express negatively the extremity of convulsive effort which
was his life:

> Γνῶθι σεαυτόν! [Know thyself!]—and is this the prime
> And heaven-sprung adage of the olden time!—
> Say, canst thou make thyself? Learn first that trade—
> Haply thou mayst know what thyself had made.
> What hast thou, Man, that thou dar'st call thine own?—
> What is there in thee, Man, that can be known?—
> Dark fluxion, all unfixable by thought,
> A phantom dim of past and future wrought,
> Vain sister of the worm,—life, death, soul, clod—
> Ignore thyself, and strive to know thy God!
>
> (*Self-knowledge*)

TWO

William Wordsworth

MILITANT QUIETIST

For contemplation hee and valour form'd.
—Milton

Two Natures

*I*n one of his passages of self-analysis in *The Prelude*, Wordsworth speaks about

> Having two natures in me (joy the one,
> The other melancholy), and withal
> A happy man, and therefore bold to look
> On painful things. . . .

(X, 868)

It is easy to see why this great heir (and rival) of Milton had a special affection, as it seems, for *L'Allegro* and *Il Penseroso*: he recognized himself in both poems; he was the Mirthful Man and the Melancholy Man together. Nevertheless—"withal"— he was "a happy man"—we must not think that his joyous side (the happy-hearted Natural Man) warred destructively with his somber, melancholy side (the Pensive or Meditative or Contemplative Man). No, as Milton's poems are companion pieces which balance each other in a happy match of contradiction, unite harmoniously in a kind of duet or *pas de deux* of contrary dispositions, so, Wordsworth tells us, do his two opposing sides join together to make the happy poet. He was no Coleridge condemned to waste his days "in querulous lassitude."* In him self-division was *not* a disease.

---

* At the end of Book X of *The Prelude*, which Wordsworth was completing in the latter part of 1804, he hopes for Coleridge, who was then in Sicily, that his

Yet there is a big difference between Milton and Wordsworth. *L'Allegro* and *Il Penseroso*, as variations on the tradi-
tionally opposed Renaissance idealities of Profane Love and
Sacred Love, this world's Nature and the other world's Spirit,
compose an elegant balancing act; as a confident Renaissance
harmonization of the sensible and spiritual realms they are
full of philosophical aplomb. There is no aplomb in Wordsworth. His opposite-leaning inclinations to joy and gloom,
which he declares so baldly and as baldly resolves, constitute
a division rooted in the poet's nerves, not in his conceptions;
they make two *natures*. There is nothing anxious or problematic about Milton's paradox of the Cheerful Sociability of sense
and the Solitary Pensiveness of spirit, because it rests on the
solid ground of a still unbroken religious confidence. But the
paradoxical Wordsworth happiness is an in-spite-of condition
of the soul, in spite of a nature split in two, and must somehow accommodate the split, combine or blend the two parts;
so it is edged with uneasiness. In the revised version of the
passage in the 1850 *Prelude*, a much older Wordsworth, now
perhaps feeling uncomfortable about confessing to a melancholy *nature* (or just forgetting how it had been with him),
abolishes the antithesis, with the result that his happiness
changes from paradoxical-anxious to bland: now Wordsworth
describes himself, quite unexceptionally, as being "somewhat
stern / In temperament," yet "withal a happy man."

The young Wordsworth's being a happy man had the strange
consequence, as he describes it, of leading him into moral despair, into the worst mental crisis he ever had to endure. The
crisis began early in 1793 when England was drawn into the

---

stay there will be as a "visitant" and a "votary"
    And not as a captive pining for his home
    In querulous lassitude.
But this last phrase described Coleridge's habitual state too well, and Wordsworth dropped it from the text.

war against revolutionary France. By that time Wordsworth had paid two visits to France and had become an "active partisan" (as he calls himself in *The Prelude*) of the revolutionary cause and the universal salvation it promised through the reign of liberty; he had also become the lover of a Frenchwoman. Yet he remained in most respects a countrified English youth, rather more insular than less, who retained an innocent confidence that his native land would always be found on the side of liberty. The outbreak of the war, coming just after Wordsworth had been forced by lack of cash to quit France and Annette Vallon and return home, shocked him violently. "Hitherto," Mrs. Moorman writes, "his love for his homeland had marched step for step with his new love for France and for humanity; now they were torn violently apart."[1] Turning against his own people, rejoicing at the news of English defeats, the young man who was already the lover of a foreign woman repudiated his dearest feelings for the country and the countryside that had formed him and became "A patriot of the world"* (*Prel.* [1850] X, 242). Till then Wordsworth's unreflective youthful hopes and confidence had been basis enough for his faith in the revolutionary cause. But now he needed something solider, conclusions which had been reasoned out and could not be impeached, and he looked for these to the rationalist ideas current among the English political radicals, to

the philosophy
That promised to abstract the hopes of men

*In becoming a cosmopolitan, Wordsworth went against his own nature and embraced the "unnatural self" that he subsequently shakes off in the opening lines of *The Prelude*. Writing on November 7, 1794, to his friend William Mathews, with whom he had hoped to publish a periodical to be called *The Philanthropist*, the cosmopolitan Wordsworth could express himself as "unnaturally" as in the following: "I begin to wish much to be in town; cataracts and mountains are good occasional society, but they will not do for constant companions."

Out of his feelings, to be fixed thenceforth
For ever in a purer element.

(Prel. X, 807)

It was in these circumstances of moral and intellectual up-
heaval, with his mind "let loose and goaded" by the "shock
[that] had been given / To old opinions," that Wordsworth
undertook a searching inquiry, the painfulness of which he
likens to surgery, into the first foundations and final justification of all moral and social belief. He was able to undertake
such an inquiry, he writes, because as a man of essentially
happy character he dared "to look on painful things"; and
daring in this way he landed up in despair:

> A happy man, and therefore bold to look
> On painful things—slow, somewhat, too, and stern
> In temperament—I took the knife in hand,
> And, stopping not at parts less sensitive,
> Endeavoured with my best of skill to probe
> The living body of society
> Even to the heart. I pushed without remorse
> My speculations forward, yea, set foot
> On Nature's holiest places.

"Dragging all passions, notions, shapes of faith, / Like cul-
prits to the bar," he challenged the mind to justify "in plain
day / Her titles and her honors," all her claims to knowledge:

> now believing,
> Now disbelieving, endlessly perplexed
> With impulse, motive, right and wrong, the ground
> Of moral obligation—what the rule,
> And what the sanction—till, demanding proof,
> And seeking it in every thing, I lost
> All feeling of conviction, and, in fine,

Sick, wearied out with contrarieties,
Yielded up moral questions in despair.

(X, 870)

This is a very different history from Coleridge's. Coleridge was better acquainted with despair than Wordsworth, yet not quite with what Wordsworth here calls "moral" despair. Moral despair Coleridge recoiled from in a panic; he would never push *his* speculations so far as to risk his Christian faith. That was the one source of consolation which remained to him. As Carlyle quotes Coleridge as saying about himself, he only "*skirted* the howling deserts of Infidelity."[2] Wordsworth's explanation for Coleridge's timidity of thought about fundamental matters of faith, implied in what he says about himself, is that as an unhappy man Coleridge lacked the inner strength to examine boldly into the foundations of his convictions. After the two men quarrelled, so Crabb Robinson reports, Wordsworth said that "no man has completely understood him—Coleridge not excepted, who is not happy enough to enter into his feelings. 'I am myself,' said he, 'one of the happiest of men, and no man who does not partake of that happiness, who lives a life of constant bustle, and whose felicity depends on the opinions of others, can possibly comprehend the best of my poems.'"[3]

For one of the happiest of men, this sounds pretty angry.* Wordsworth is smarting from the bad, even insulting reception his poems were getting in those years, and smarting too from the quarrel with Coleridge. Stiff with resentment, he attacks the understanding of the man who was his first and

---

*Another angry claimant to the knowledge of true happiness is Yeats:
  Because this age and the next age
  Engender in the ditch,
  No man can know a happy man
  From any passing wretch.

(*The Old Stone Cross*)

most perceptive supporter, on the grounds that Coleridge is too dependent on the busyness of London literary life and other people's good opinion to appreciate the quietudes and exaltations of his poetry of solitude. Behind the injustice of his words, however, lies the truth which Coleridge, not Wordsworth, was the first to express (which Coleridge *rushed* to express in the first days of their friendship): that he, Wordsworth, is strong in himself and his sole spirit, and Coleridge weak and necessitous.

To be sure, the state of moral despair that Wordsworth describes himself as falling into resembles the Hamlet state, though rather the one described by Schlegel than by Coleridge: the state of mind of a Hamlet who "loses himself in labyrinths of thought in which neither end nor beginning is discoverable," of a *Hamlet* in which "the destiny of humanity is exhibited as a gigantic Sphinx, which threatens to precipitate into the abyss of scepticism all who are unable to solve her dreadful enigmas." [4] But it isn't because his nature is too weak—too introverted or too idealistic or too sensitive or somehow crippled—that he nearly breaks down mentally. His strength, not weakness—his moral courage, deliberation, and sternness of resolve—is responsible for the drastic lengths to which he pushes his reasonings. It is Wordsworth's own strong character, when employed in

> reasonings false
> From the beginning, inasmuch as drawn
> Out of a heart which had been turned aside
> From Nature,
>
> (*Prel.* X, 883)

which brings about the moral crisis. Coleridge, giving up on life, retired into his mind; it was a retreat. Wordsworth advances into his mind to challenge her titles and her honors; it is an attack. Coleridge took refuge from the pains of living life, from thinking about what he needs must feel, in a life-

long death-in-life of thinking about abstractions and generalizations. But it is for the sake of living his life, so as to establish his actions on a solid basis, that Wordsworth wrestles
with the perplexities of

> Impulse, motive, right and wrong, the ground
> Of moral obligation—what the rule
> And what the sanction.

Even in his worst time nature did not suspend the ministry
she performed for him:

> I saw the spring return, when I was dead
> To deeper hope, yet had I joy for her
> And welcomed her benevolence.
>
> (*Prel.* XI, 24)

Coleridge in his worst times, oppressed by "A grief without
a pang, void, dark, and drear, / A stifled drowsy, unimpas-
sioned grief," could gaze at the evening sky with its thin
clouds, its now sparkling now bedimmed stars and crescent
moon, but

> I see them all so excellently fair,
> I see, not feel, how beautiful they are!
>
> (*Dejection*)

In all this Wordsworth was rather an anti-Hamlet adventuring
into the forests of the mind to do battle with the Hamlet
demon of doubtfulness, but temporarily overthrown by his
adversary.

Wordsworth's account of this crisis in *The Prelude* is ambiva-
lent. As a happy man and therefore bold to look on painful
things, he *took a knife to the living body of society*; he *pushed his
speculations forward without remorse*; he *set foot on Nature's holiest
places*. His knife-wielding militancy of mind is cruel and sacrilegious and doesn't stop at probing the social body even to the
heart. At the same time, his daring to probe the social body
even to the heart has the sound of something surgical, radical,

heroic. Of course there is a distinction here: the rationalism is cruel and sacrilegious, while the spiritual militancy is only misemployed, "misguided and misguiding." When Wordsworth recovers his life in nature and his poet's vocation, his militancy, henceforth employed in poetry, will show itself as visionary power, the Wordsworthian sublime. And yet the distinction is oddly blurred in the passage. It is there logically but not emotionally. The good of moral and intellectual intrepidity and assertion is all mixed up with the bad of sacrilegiousness, violence, and overstepping limits.

All his life Wordsworth had a good opinion of his own character; he liked himself. In *The Prelude* he describes this character as being Miltonically militant, exalted, stern:

> A rock with torrents roaring, with the clouds
> Familiar, and a favorite of the stars.

> (XIII, 231)

The only fault he finds with it is that it is overstern. Like Milton, when Wordsworth was a revolutionary he approved the killing of a king. Like Milton, he was ready to "suffer the most atrocious doctrines to be recommended" rather than restrict freedom of inquiry and discussion. "Let nothing be deemed too sacred for investigation," he wrote Mathews on June 8, 1794. Afterwards he didn't turn upon these things, and himself, in disgust and chagrin; the crisis he went through was a crisis of disorientation and defeat of his moral and intellectual energies and aspirations, not a crisis of self-repudiation.

Nevertheless, as he looked back on this first venture of his militant spirit in which he went so far astray from nature, he was unsure if militancy of spirit wasn't overweeningness, violence, transgression. The serpent tempts Eve in *Paradise Lost* by telling her that till he tasted the "fair Apples" of the Tree of Forbidden Knowledge he had been a beast of the field, with nothing on his mind but food and sex; but having eaten,

> to Speculations high or deep
> I turned my thoughts, and with capacious mind

Considered all things visible in Heav'n,
Or Earth, or Middle, all things fair and good.

(IX, 602)

Milton's (and Wordsworth's) idea of knowledge is our civilization's Faustian one that knowledge of good and evil is knowledge of *all* things, both good and evil. The Tree in Eden is not
a narrowly ethical plant; nor, therefore, is sin narrowly ethical. When Adam and Eve eat the fruit of knowledge, with
Satanic presumption they

fancy that they feel
Divinity within them breeding wings
Wherewith to scorn the earth.

(IX, 1009)

After the visionary enthusiasm of his days as a revolutionary
rationalist had ended in a breakdown or something close to it,
that was what Wordsworth was always afraid of—scorning the
earth. But at the same time he was also afraid of *not* scorning
the earth—of falling into what *Tintern Abbey* calls "the dreary
intercourse of daily life," of becoming loaded down with the
"earthly freight" which in the *Immortality Ode* weighs upon
the soul soon enough, crushing it. His imagination stooped
with some self-consciousness to incidents and situations of
common life in the *Lyrical Ballads*; its natural tendency was
to soar.

Wordsworth didn't apologize when writing *The Prelude* for
having been a partisan of the French Revolution. * On the contrary: it had been bliss to be alive in the revolutionary dawn
when the whole earth wore the beauty of promise. He had
been mistaken in his hope that man, by abstracting his reason
out of his feelings and elevating it into some purer sphere,
might arrive at "a secure intelligence" on the basis of which it
would be possible for a higher human nature to unfold itself;

---

*But as time passed he gradually forgot how he had been a revolutionary. It
was as if it all had to do with somebody else.

but he had not been mistaken in hoping for a higher nature, in hoping for man to

> start
> Out of the worm-like state* in which he is,
> And spread abroad the wings of Liberty,
> Lord of himself, in undisturbed delight.

No, that remained a noble aspiration:

> A noble aspiration!—yet I feel
> The aspiration—but with other thoughts
> And happier: for I was perplexed and sought
> To accomplish the transition by such means
> As did not lie in nature.

> (*Prel.* X, 835)

His hope as a poet is still his old hope as a revolutionary, that mankind, growing wings, might rise aloft into a higher sphere. But man has to stick to nature to bring about this transition†; Wordsworth fears to scorn the earth. Of course, *higher sphere* may mean—perhaps *must* mean—"out of nature," beyond nature, scorning the earth. Wordsworth, however, refuses to consider this. He is going to have it both ways: nature *and* a higher nature. His visionary militancy carries him aloft into the heavens; sometimes it carries him higher than the heavens, past

> Jehovah—with his thunder, and the choir
> Of shouting Angels, and the empyreal thrones

into worlds "To which the Heaven of Heavens is but a veil." And yet these farthest worlds, these ultimate regions are only

---

*In the 1850 *Prelude* Wordsworth says "*earthy*, worm-like state." The word *earth* has an ambiguous meaning for him: it is man's appointed place in nature, and yet man is called upon to rise above his earthy nature, which is too wormlike. In the *Immortality Ode* the earth is only a "homely Nurse" to her "Foster-child" man, who is a prince in exile.

†Man has to stick to nature and Wordsworth has to stick to England, to English particularity (and insularity) as against French universality, to an English wife.

the heights and depths of his own mind, that "discerning intellect of Man" which, "When wedded to this goodly universe / In love and holy passion, shall find" the Paradisal higher sphere "A simple produce of the common day" (*Home at Grasmere*, 782–808).

At the end of *The Prelude* Wordsworth says about himself that "even till the very going-out of youth," till he was almost thirty,

> I too exclusively esteemed that love,
> And sought that beauty, which as Milton sings
> Hath terror in it.
>
> (XIII, 224)

What he is deploring in himself is his too marked inclination to the sublime, to the thin inhuman air of the mountain heights and farthest reaches of supernal vision. That is, he is deploring his too marked inclination to Miltonism. Milton didn't worry about Miltonism because his heavenly heights were still firmly connected with the earth (in *Paradise Lost*, by a golden chain). Milton's unearthliness consists in his confident command of the Divine perspective; he knows what God thinks: as Paul says, "For the Spirit explores everything, even the depths of God's own nature. . . . We . . . possess the mind of Christ" (1 Cor. 2:10–16). At such a height of vision the ordinary human life of earth looks pretty small; it plays little part in a poem scaled to first and last and midst and without end. *Paradise Lost*, though insisting with its biblical spirituality on the highest worth of the common life, is not much concerned with it. Yet Milton isn't afraid for one minute of losing his footing on the earth, of being lost to human life. *
His cosmic muse Urania is a safe guide:

> Up led by thee
> Into the Heaven of Heavens I have presumed,

---

* Anti-Miltonists think he should be. Their complaint is that he is not like Shakespeare, not human: remote in his vision from the life of men and remote in his verse from the speech of men.

An Earthly Guest, and drawn Empyreal Air,
Thy tempering; with like safety guided down
Return me to my Native Element.

(VII, 12)

He expresses fear, not of falling *out* of human life but of falling
back into it, like Bellerophon, unable to sustain the unex-
ampled flight. Milton is at home in sublimity. At the start of
Book VII he experiences some relief at being back in his native
element—

Standing on Earth, not rapt above the Pole,
More safe I sing with mortal voice

—but this is by way of introduction to singing the Creation!
Singing the Creation of the World and the Fall of Man is a
down-to-earth matter for him, not a cosmic trip like the far-
out ("Empyreal") War in Heaven whose story he has just told,
which really strained his "mortal voice"! Wordsworth's case
is quite different. His heights (or depths) are unexplored regions (of the Mind of Man), without an established relation to
the earth. Soaring past Jehovah and the Heaven of Heavens,
outdoing even Milton as he thinks, he runs the risk of never
getting back to earth—like his own Newton "for ever / Voy-
aging through strange seas of Thought, alone" (*Prel.* [1850]
III, 62).

Against the dangers of Miltonism Wordsworth turns to
Milton, to Raphael's advice to Adam to

be lowly wise:
Think only what concerns thee and thy being;
Dream not of other worlds,

(VIII, 173)

and to Adam's advice to himself:

to know
That which before us lies in daily life,

Is the prime Wisdom.*

(VIII, 192)

Wordsworth studied to be lowly wise. His quietism, as well
as being a countertendency of his nature, was the moral-
imaginative effort of a mighty poet following the Miltonic
counsel of his own "deliberate Voice" of reason in *Home at
Grasmere*: "Be mild and cleave to gentle things." Yet in spite
of Milton he still continues to dream, Miltonically and sub-
limely, of other worlds. He pursues the prodigy of human redemption *through* the platitude of nature; for by cleaving to
the ordinary things of earth as to a spouse, by marrying his
far-ranging "intellect of Man" to the nature which before us
lies in daily life, he hopes to rebuild Paradise out of "nothing
more than what we are":

> Paradise, and groves
> Elysian, Fortunate Fields—like those of old
> Sought in the Atlantic Main—why should they be
> A history only of departed things,
> Or a mere fiction of what never was?
> For the discerning intellect of Man,
> When wedded to this goodly Universe
> In love and holy passion, shall find these
> A simple produce of the common day.
> —I, long before the blissful hour arrives,
> Would chant, in lonely peace, the spousal verse
> Of this great consummation:—and by words
> Which speak of nothing more than what we are,
> Would I arouse the sensual from their sleep

---

*Miltonism and Milton are balanced in Wordsworth's sonnet on him:
  Thy soul was like a Star, and dwelt apart;
  Thou hadst a voice whose soul was like the sea:
  Pure as the naked heavens, majestic, free,
  So didst thou travel on life's common way,
  In cheerful godliness; and yet thy heart
  The lowliest duties on herself did lay.

Of Death, and win the vacant and the vain
To noble raptures.

(*Home at Grasmere*, 800)

There is a heart of paradox in Wordsworth's work. And it comes—in part—from his having been a stubborn, determined man who insisted on having it both ways: both this world as it is and this world as it isn't. The great Wordsworthian paradox consists in the marriage of heaven and earth, of the militant sublime mind and mild material nature, of the high-flying poetry of the imagination and the creeping prose of daily life. But it cost Wordsworth an enormous inner effort to live a paradox, the oxymoron of Militant Quietism, and after a while he couldn't. Militant quietism was the "wise"—that is, active—"passiveness" of the "feeling mind" (or "thinking heart") in "that serene and blessed mood" (to shift from *Expostulation and Reply* to *Hart-leap Well* to *Tintern Abbey*) in which taking in is also giving forth, perception is imagination (creation), and the mind becomes "a *living* soul."

But this is a hard mood to sustain; in fact, it can't be sustained as a *mood*. What gradually took its place was a passive passiveness, a stubborn apatheticalness, a repudiation of desire and emotion, energy and assertion. This expressed itself in often eloquent scoldings, as in the fine first sonnet of Wordsworth's quartet attacking *Personal Talk*, almost funny in its general air of rudeness. In this sonnet Wordsworth says how he would rather sit in "barren silence" than converse in the ordinary way of life—the oppressive, irritating, boring ordinary way of life—with friends and neighbors:

Better than such discourse doth silence long,
Long, barren silence, square with my desire;
To sit without emotion, hope, or aim,
By my half-kitchen and half-parlour fire,*

---

*I quote Wordsworth's earlier, preferred, and preferable version of this line, which describes the location of the fireplace in Dove Cottage.

> And listen to the flapping of the flame,
> Or kettle whispering its faint undersong.

To live without emotion, hope, or aim is quietism with a ven-geance, to the death. Sometimes in his latter days Wordsworth revived the two terms of the paradox—heaven-storming mili-tancy and earth-hugging quiet—but the paradox itself, with its difficult literal effort, was gone, its place taken by ordinary sententiousness. Such is the skylark poem already referred to—a fine piece of verse, complete with one of his spectacular lines ("A privacy of glorious light is thine"), yet touched with some complacency in its reconciliation of the human and the more-than-human spheres by an easy formula: "Type of the wise who soar, but never roam; / True to the kindred points of Heaven and Home."

Wordsworth was cured of his spiritual distemper by going back to his first life in the north of England countryside, by recovering the feelings of his earlier life: "Nature's self," as-sisted by the steady presence of his sister and then by his new friend Coleridge, led him back

> through the weary labyrinth
> . . . to open day,
> Revived the feelings of my earlier life,
> Gave me that strength and knowledge full of peace,
> Enlarged, and never more to be disturbed.
>
> (*Prel.* X, 921)

Nature gave him knowledge full of peace, but there was more "disturbance" in the knowledge than he wished to allow. Wordsworth came back *seeking* nature's peace and there was disturbance in the very effort. The simple poet of the early, unselfconscious, heroic ages, as Schiller says, *is* nature; but the "sentimental"—or self-conscious and reflective—poet of modern times must strive after it with post-Adamic discon-tent. Wordsworth emerged from "the weary labyrinth" a reflective man, a man who had been moved to think about himself. *That* disturbance in his soul ended only with his life. If at first he considers himself a neophyte in introspection, saying to Coleridge,

> Thou, my friend, art one
> More deeply read in thy own thoughts,
>
> (*Prel.* II, 215)

by the time he gets to the end of the 1850 *Prelude* he is calling himself a "self-haunting spirit"—a phrase which could just as easily be applied to the mind-oppressed Coleridge.*

The phrase indeed occurs in a passage in which Wordsworth thanks the influence of Coleridge ("O capacious Soul! / Placed on this earth to love and understand") for the fact that

> thoughts and things
> In the self-haunting spirit learned to take
> More rational proportions; mystery,
> The incumbent mystery of sense and soul,
> Of life and death, time and eternity,
> Admitted more habitually a mild
> Interposition—a serene delight
> In closelier gathering cares, such as become
> A human creature, howsoe'er endowed,
> Poet, or destined for a humbler name.
>
> (*Prel.* [1850] XIV, 283)

Wordsworth is thanking his Hamletish friend, that is, for having helped to preserve him from Hamletism—from becoming too much occupied with an inner world of sublime thoughts, to the neglect of life and the practical cares of life such as become the human creature. Though Wordsworth understands Hamletism according to the Coleridge formula as an im-

---

*H. M. Margoliouth says that "Coleridge taught him introspection" (*Wordsworth and Coleridge 1795–1834* [1953], 35). Wordsworth's vigorous "outness" of nature needed to be taught it, but as a modern spirit Wordsworth took readily to the teaching.

balance between "thoughts and things," the danger he sees in it is that of a proud sublimity of mind inhumanly exalted above the earth and earthly concerns into a philosophical-religious empyrean. There is nothing in it of Coleridge's horror of a limbo state of inanition and paralysis, of a "crepuscular half-being," of the "spirit-jail" of the "blank Naught-at-all." The danger in Hamletism for Wordsworth indeed is not too much horror but too much joy, though a special kind of joy, the too enthusiastic delight of the Pensive Man in the solitary, ontological contemplation of nature. Wordsworth owed it to Coleridge, he wrote, that

> the deep enthusiastic joy,
> The rapture of the hallelujah sent
> From all that breathes and is, was chastened, stemmed,
> And balanced, by a reason which indeed
> Is reason, duty, and pathetic truth—
> And God and man divided, as they ought,
> Between them the great system of the world
> Where man is sphered, and which God animates.
>
> (XIII, 261)

God and man divide the world "as they ought," as is metaphysically and morally right and proper. His self-haunting spirit, Wordsworth says, threatened this division; if unchecked, it would have drawn him out of man's sphere over into an inhuman one, into a ghostly poetry hailing the superhuman with a mouth that has no moisture and no breath.

Wordsworth's is still a divided nature, with the uneasiness of such, but withal he is a happy man—warned by Coleridge, and by Coleridge's example, he has learned to keep a due balance between thoughts and things and thus preserved himself from a spirituality that leaves human life behind.

Was Wordsworth happy? The miserable Coleridge would have laughed at such a question—for him Wordsworth was the definition of happiness! Nevertheless, the poet whose mind brooded over the thought of mighty poets in their misery dead, suffered from attacks of despondency all his life. In a sense, Coleridge taught Wordsworth that he was a happy man. Of course he did not teach him to *feel* happy; he taught him that his nature was so constituted as to establish him in the state of happiness; he taught him the psycho-philosophical *idea* of his happiness. Till Wordsworth met Coleridge he seems not to have thought about himself very much; his main attention was directed outward, upon the world. But the world had given him pause and he was ready to look inward. Meeting Coleridge, who was so much interested in himself (as well as in Wordsworth), awakened Wordsworth's interest in himself—though not so much in himself as *him*self, but in himself as a more or less impersonal register of his sensations and intuitions of relationship with the world standing over against him. The poet of the Egotistical Sublime never had much interest in his personal self.

With a roast-beef contempt for abstractions, Wordsworth disdained ideas, ideas as such. In old age he thanked Heaven he had never read a word of German metaphysics. Yet the modern poetry of self-reflection, which he was one of the inaugurators of, could not do without ideas, and he especially could not do without an idea of himself which would help to organize his sensations and intuitions. Wordsworth got that idea from his friend. Wordsworth's *idea* of himself is Coleridge's idea of him, and Coleridge's idea of him is that he is *not* Coleridge, not Hamletish, not morbidly sunk in himself and his own thoughts, at the cost of his life. Of course I don't mean Wordsworth got his sense of self from his friend; by the idea of himself I mean a certain explicit consciousness of himself. The Coleridge and Wordsworth one finds vis-à-vis one another in *The Prelude* are Coleridge and Wordsworth as Coleridge understood himself and Wordsworth, essentially.

Thus Wordsworth (following Coleridge), describes Coleridge as having grown up in London where his youth, because "Debarred from Nature's living images," had been passed in the "airy wretchedness" of a sickly, insubstantial mental life, a life of

> subtle speculations, toils abstruse
> Among the schoolmen, and Platonic forms
> Of wild ideal pageantry, shaped out
> From things well-matched, or ill, and words for things—
> The self-created sustenance of a mind
> Debarred from Nature's living images,
> Compelled to be a life unto itself.

(VI, 308)

He, Wordsworth, however, had grown up in a solid natural world, not pining in the abstract city, his mind steadied and controlled by concrete realities:

> I had forms distinct
> To steady me. [My] thoughts did oft revolve
> About some centre palpable, which at once
> Incited them to motion, and controlled,
>   . . . I still
> At all times had a real solid world
> Of images about me, did not pine
> As one in cities bred might do—as thou,
> Beloved friend, hast told me that thou didst,
> Great spirit as thou art—in endless dreams
> Of sickliness, disjoining, joining, things
> Without the light of knowledge.

(VIII, 598)

Wordsworth learned from Coleridge to make this claim for himself; and what he is claiming for himself is precisely what Coleridge disclaimed for Hamlet and himself: "a due balance between our attention to outward objects and our meditation on inward thoughts—a due balance between the real and the imaginary world." [5] Wordsworth claimed indeed not only a balance but a *unity* of thoughts and things, mind and world. The foundations of his mind (he writes about the Pedlar—that is, himself) had been laid in circumstances in which thoughts were hardly less substantial than things, in which

> deep feelings had impressed
> Great objects on his mind with portraiture
> And colour so distinct that on his mind
> They lay like substances, and almost seemed
> To haunt the bodily sense.

Before his ninth year, watching the sun rise from the tops of mountains and bathe in light the ocean, earth, and sky, he had read in the silent spectacle "unutterable love":

> Sound needed none,
> Nor any voice of joy: his spirit drank
> The spectacle. Sensation, soul and form
> All melted into him. They swallowed up
> His animal being. In them did he live,
> And by them did he live. They were his life.
> In such access of mind, in such high hour
> Of visitation from the living God,
> He did not feel the God, he felt his works.
> Thought was not: in enjoyment it expired.[6]

Nature is no longer nature, mind mind; there is only perfect unity. But to be able to describe it so, to be the poet of such experience, requires self-conscious thought; and such self-conscious reflection exploded a unity in which everything had been swallowed up and thought was not. Wordsworth discovered that as his poet's mind grew in him and fathered glorious verse, in the same measure the glorious being he had known passed away from him. Nevertheless, although his recollection of that sense of unity changed in a few years' time from ecstatic into elegiac, into a recognition of how much had been lost, enough remained for happiness: there was the primal sympathy which having been once must ever be; and there was the philosophic mind itself, which the years bring, to console him for his fall into philosophy.

The Wordsworthian happiness was closely bound up with the state of solitude—it was not to be found among the crowds of men in cities. Wordsworth was a solitary. But again it was probably Coleridge who taught him to understand this so distinctly about himself; again it was a case, for Coleridge, of Wordsworth's being so very much, so supremely, not-Coleridge. "I own myself no self-subsisting Mind," Coleridge wrote in 1804. "I know, I feel, that I am weak—apt to faint away inwardly, self-deserted & bereft of the confidence in my own powers—and that the approbation & Sympathy of good & intelligent men is my Sea-breeze, without which I should languish from Morn to evening."[7] Wordsworth on the other hand *was* a self-subsisting mind, a rock of self-sufficiency, one who from the first had dwelt in "the dread watch-tower of man's absolute self," as Coleridge put it in his poem *To William Wordsworth*. "He is *all* man," he is reported in the *Table Talk* as saying about Wordsworth; "he is a man of whom it might have been said, 'It is good for him to be alone.'"[8] There is, however, the implication that Wordsworth, not needing sympathy himself, lacked it for others. He felt indeed a powerful "sympathy with man as man," Coleridge wrote in the *Biographia Literaria*, but it was that "of a contemplator" standing apart "rather than a fellow-sufferer or co-mate."[9] When Wordsworth told Crabb Robinson in 1812 that he was "one of the happiest of men," and that neither Coleridge nor any man "who lives a life of constant bustle, and whose felicity depends on the opinions of others" could possibly understand his best poems, he was praising himself and dispraising Coleridge in terms which he had learned from Coleridge. Though he was well aware of his intellectual debt to Coleridge, in his unawareness of more personal things he had a smack of country coarseness.

Yet there was a lot of uneasiness for Wordsworth, and more than a touch of contradiction, in a happiness based on solitude; and this makes his declaration that he was "one of the happiest of men" hollow-sounding. He was man alone. But it is *not* good for man to be alone. Wordsworth acknowledged this by striving to go out of himself, by trying to show how "Love of Nature Lead[s] to Love of Mankind" (the title of Book VIII of *The Prelude*), by marrying and founding a family and embracing social duties. He says about himself in Book II that he had been "taught to feel, perhaps too much, / The self-sufficing power of Solitude" (77). In that quintessential Wordsworthian poem *To Joanna*, which addresses his future sister-in-law Joanna Hutchinson as one who learned "amid the smoke of cities" to love the living beings by her own fireside, he calls Dorothy and himself, who live among the woods and fields and make friends with the streams and groves, "transgressors." Five years later *Elegiac Stanzas* breaks violently with Wordsworthian nature. What had seemed its "Elysian quiet," without toil or strife, its "steadfast peace" and benignity, he now calls an "illusion"; he says remorsefully that the death of his brother at sea has finally "humanized" his soul, and he repudiates a happiness based on inhuman nature solitudes:

> Farewell, farewell the heart that lives alone,
> Housed in a dream, at distance from the Kind!
> Such happiness, wherever it be known,
> Is to be pitied; for 'tis surely blind.

Yet he remained a man alone.

Wordsworth's temper as a young man was restless, vehement, ambitious. It drove him out of the parochial circumstances of his childhood to Cambridge, to London, to France. But this restlessness led to self-betrayal (as he subsequently deemed it) when he became a cosmopolitan and a patriot of the world, filled with revolutionary ambitions to save it. In his long retreat out of the storm of universal history which had swept him off his feet, he finally came to rest at Grasmere with his sister at the end of 1799. It was a conscious withdrawal from the world, even though he had not yet quite turned thirty. In an excluded passage of *Home at Grasmere*, the poem which describes his settling down there, he calls Dorothy and himself "A pair seceding from the common world." [10] And yet for him it was a case of *reculer pour mieux sauter*. For his forward-thrusting, adventurous spirit, in finding its home at Grasmere, did not in fact give up its ambitious designs upon the world, to redeem it. *Home at Grasmere* is the poem whose concluding section is the heaven-storming verses Wordsworth published separately years later as a "Prospectus" of the great philosophical epic he still meant to write "On Man, On Nature, and on Human Life" (to quote the first line of those verses)—verses which sound the most ambitious epic note in all his poetry. His militant spirit now asserts itself in poetry, not in French Revolutions, and demands to know why Paradise should only be an ancient story and not the everyday reality—though a too exalted poetry ran the risk of losing touch with the earth just as his too abstracted revolutionary rationalism had done.

Wordsworth began writing *Home at Grasmere* in 1800, in his first days in that valley. At last he had made a start (if only a start) on the monumental philosophical epic he and Coleridge had talked about with so much excitement (with more excitement than definite understanding, at least on Wordsworth's part*); for *Home at Grasmere* was slated by him to be the introductory first book of the main part of "The Recluse." However, the long work that preempted his imagination during the next years (till 1805), as it turned out, was not the philo-

---

* As far as Coleridge was concerned, the plan of "The Recluse" couldn't have been clearer. The poem was to be "in substance, what I have been all my life doing in my system of philosophy," he remarked many years later in conversation (*Table Talk*, July 21, 1832). But Wordsworth may be forgiven for having found what Coleridge called his "system" less clear, as matter for poetry, than it was to its author as philosophical matter—all the more so as the philosopher got no further along in the *systematic* exposition of his philosophy than the poet did in composing his philosophical poem.

sophical epic but the psycho-philosophical autobiography of
his first twenty-seven years, which he had begun writing in
Germany in the winter of 1798–99. That poem began, in-
genuously and undeliberately, as an effort to see why getting
started with "The Recluse" was proving such a baffling thing
to him. Had all the forces which had conspired to make him
what he was, all that "fair seed-time," only labored to produce
this dumbness, this indolence, this impotence? "Was it for
this," he exclaims in lines which were *The Prelude*'s primitive
beginning,

> That one, the fairest of all rivers, loved
> To blend his murmurs with my nurse's song,
> And from his alder shades and rocky falls,
> And from his fords and shallows, sent a voice
> That flowed along my dreams?

(Prel. I, 271)

As Wordsworth pursued the poem about himself further
and further, still without getting on to the great philosophical
poem, he justified his preoccupation with the memory poem
by thinking of it as a part of "The Recluse," first as its tail-
piece and then as its preamble. But after finishing *The Prelude*
in 1805, when he turned again to his main, his epic task, he
found his bafflement before it just as strong as ever. Nor was
Coleridge, sunk in misery and feelings of defeat, any help
now; that fountain had ceased to flow for him. It wasn't till
1814, nine years after he had finished *The Prelude*, that Wordsworth published *The Excursion*, offering it to the public as the
"intermediate part" of "The Recluse." He would have preferred publishing the philosophical part first, if that had been
written, but it hadn't. However, at long last here was a piece of
his long-thought-about great work on Man, Nature and Society, even if it wasn't the main piece; and to give some idea of
what he meant to do in "The Recluse" as a whole, he quoted
in his preface to *The Excursion* the great dithyramb of 107 lines
which concluded the unpublished *Home at Grasmere*. But the

contrast between the "Prospectus of the Recluse" offered in the preface and the long poem which follows it is extreme. What *The Excursion* doesn't have is just the driving epic energy, the poetic militancy of the "Prospectus." The latter flashes and rocks as with lightning and thunder; its quality is what the eighteenth century called "terrific." The last word you would apply to *The Excursion* is *terrific*.

You feel that Wordsworth quotes the long passage out of *Home at Grasmere* more elegiacally than prospectively, to show what he *might* have done, what he had wished to do, as Milton's successor. For now in 1814, long years after the enthusiastic days of his collaboration with Coleridge, his hopes for his great work, and for an old-time greatness for himself as the author of a great work, were beginning to wear thin. All during Wordsworth's life as a poet, "The Recluse" confronted him as an immediate task, spoiling his contentment. The consequence of this (to adapt the mot of Helen Darbyshire) was that *everything* he wrote had for him, however faintly, the character either of a prelude to or an excursion from his main endeavor—till he gave the whole thing up in his last years. So in Wordsworth's life, too, though he accomplished so much, there was the Coleridgian pang for what had not been achieved, the haunting Hamlet sense of being baffled and stopped from doing what he felt so powerfully called upon to do.*

Home at Grasmere was never published in Wordsworth's lifetime. His failure to write "The Recluse" must have involved

---

*The Harvard professor George Ticknor had dinner with the Wordsworths in 1838 and had this to say about the visit in his journal:

> Mrs. Wordsworth asked me to talk to him about finishing the . . . Recluse; saying, that she could not bear to have him occupied constantly in writing sonnets and other trifles, while this great work lay by him untouched, but that she had ceased to urge him about it, therefore. He said that the Introduction [*The Prelude*], which is a sort of autobiography, is completed. This I knew, for he read me large portions of it twenty years ago. The rest is divided into three parts, the first of which is partly written in fragments, which Mr. Wordsworth says would be useless and un-

for him the failure of *Home at Grasmere*, which he saw only as an introduction to that poem. As anything else, the exultant, heroic mood of *Home at Grasmere*, its breathing a power not to be withstood, would have made the aging poet, hardening himself against the defeats of life, hesitate uncomfortably. The epic character of that mood, Wordsworth's open epical aspirations, the classical boastfulness of his epic intention are one of the most striking things about the poem's peroration:

> Urania, I shall need
> Thy guidance, or a greater Muse, if such
> Descend to earth or dwell in highest heaven!
> For I must tread on shadowy ground, must sink
> Deep—and, aloft ascending, breathe in worlds
> To which the Heaven of Heavens is but a veil.
> All strength—all terror, single or in bands,
> That ever was put forth in personal form—
> Jehovah—with his thunder, and the choir
> Of shouting Angels, and the Empyreal Thrones—
> I pass them unalarmed. Not Chaos, not
> The darkest pit of lowest Erebus,
> Nor aught of blinder vacancy, scooped out
> By help of dreams—can breed such fear and awe
> As fall upon us often when we look
> Into our minds, into the Mind of Man—
> My haunt, and the main region of my song.

"Sentimental poetry," wrote Schiller, "is born out of retirement and stillness, and invites one thereto; simple poetry is the child of life and leads one back to it." As a "sentimental" poet Wordsworth retires into the stillness of Grasmere. He recoils from the turmoil of Paris and the French Revolution, the

---

intelligible in other hands than his own; the second is the Excursion; and the third is untouched. On my asking him why he does not finish it, he turned to me very decidedly and said, "Why did not Gray finish the long poem he began on a similar subject? Because he found he had undertaken something beyond his power to accomplish. And that is my case."
—Quoted in Beth Darlington's introduction to the Cornell edition of *Home at Grasmere*, 31.

turmoil of his affair with Annette Vallon, politics, and philosophical scheming. But he isn't ready to give up on life, not at all. The life he retires from is the world's life; he has come to see that there is

> little worthy or sublime
> In what we blazon with the pompous names
> Of power and action.
>
> *(Prel.* XII, 47)

He prizes power and action as much as the simple poet does, but only as these belong to natural life and a natural humanity (he *prizes* them the more in that he prizes them self-consciously); he does not prize them as Napoleonic (modern) exercises in brutality and death. In a passage in *Home at Grasmere* that is especially full of paradox, crammed with paradox, he tries to describe what it is that pleases his soul about that "spot":

> 'tis the sense
> Of majesty, and beauty, and repose,
> A blended holiness of earth and sky,
> Something that makes this individual Spot,
> This small Abiding-place of many Men,
> A termination, and a last retreat,
> A Centre, come from wheresoe'er you will,
> A Whole without dependence or defect,
> Made for itself; and happy in itself,
> Perfect Contentment, Unity entire.

Grasmere is "Unity entire." As such it embraces everything: the majestic (sublime) and the beautiful, earth and sky, individual spot and complete whole, termination and center. Wordsworth has retreated from the world, but by turning his back on it he arrives at its very center. He is having it both ways with a vengeance.

There is a mixture of restoration and conquest ideas in his account of his return to his native countryside, of coming-home-to-rest and going-out-to-conquer feelings. When he leaves the city at the beginning of *The Prelude,** he feels like a prisoner restored to liberty "from a house of bondage"; he is a self restored to itself:

> It is shaken off,
> As by miraculous gift 'tis shaken off,
> That burthen of my own unnatural self,
> That heavy weight of many a weary day
> Not mine, and such as were not made for me.
> Long months of peace—if such bold word accord
> With any promises of human life—
> Long months of ease and undisturbed delight
> Are mine in prospect.
>
> (I, 21)

Though "the earth is all before" him at the start of *The Prelude*, as it lies before Adam and Eve at the end of *Paradise Lost*, Wordsworth is a risen not a fallen Adam. The earth is all before him not as a forbidding place of exile from Eden in which he must conquer a new home for himself, but as that very Eden and first home our first parents were driven out of, to which he is now restored "as by miraculous gift." At the very same time, however, "coming from a house of bondage" like the Jews and like them guided by "a wandering cloud"—

> and should the guide I choose
> Be nothing better than a wandering cloud
> I cannot miss my way. I breathe again—
>
> (I, 17)

he is going out to conquer Canaan. And as he breathes again, in ecstatic relief, "Trances of thought and mountings of the mind / Come fast upon" him and summon him to great ex-

---

* *The Prelude* begins at the very end of the events it narrates, with Wordsworth going back to the Lake Country to make his "Home at Grasmere." Then Wordsworth retraces the course of his earlier life. Having described in *The Prelude* the growth of his own mind and conducted the examination of his own powers as a poet, Wordsworth would then be ready to muse freely in solitude, to launch out on his meditative epic on Man, on Nature, and on Human Life.

ertions. The earth before him is a tranquil Eden, *but also* a great prospect of freedom and possibility in which he must stake out a claim for himself, the Canaan which has been appointed to him for conquest. He is *restored* to the Earthly Paradise as by miraculous gift, but only if he has the strength to *conquer* it by force of arms—by marrying the mind of man to the goodly universe in love and holy passion.

The breeze that greets the returning Wordsworth in the first lines of *The Prelude* awakens a "corresponding mild creative breeze" inside his breast. However, the latter breeze soon swells into

> A tempest, a redundant energy,
> Vexing its own creation. 'Tis a power
> That does not come unrecognized, a storm
> Which, breaking up a long-continued frost,
> Brings with it vernal promises, the hope
> Of active days, of dignity and thought,
> Of prowess in an honorable field,
> Pure passions, virtue, knowledge, and delight,
> The holy life of music and of verse.

> (I, 46)

The mild poetic afflatus awakened by the mild afflatus of nature turns into a violent tempest which "vexes" the peaceful thoughts it had inspired; the poet's mind is stirred and roused by a sense of the *power* of his imagination. The peace and undisturbed delight he had foreseen for himself is thus almost immediately disturbed by the militancy of his imagination. His mind unsteadied by this upsurge of its own strength, expressed in thoughts of possible power and accomplishment, he lies down under a tree to calm himself: "slackening my thoughts by choice, / And settling into gentler happiness" (I, 72). His deliberately relaxed thoughts are still, as he says, entirely taken up with himself; he makes up his mind to settle in the "sweet vale" of Grasmere. There, he promises himself, he will begin, and maybe even finish, "some work of glory" (that is, "The Recluse"). So his slackened thoughts have started to speed up again. But lying beneath the tree, he is

> soothed by a sense of touch
> From the warm ground, that balanced me, else lost
> Entirely, seeing nought, nought hearing, save
> When here and there about the grove of oaks
> Where was my bed, an acorn from the trees
> Fell audibly, and with a startling sound.

(I, 89)

Thoughts about power and glory, passion and prowess unnerve the poet and he must literally lie down on the ground, where the touch of the warm earth *balances* him against "losing himself entirely" in a dizzying mental empyrean of hopes and expectations. The earth soothes him, but the occasional acorn dropping loudly in the silence has perhaps a touch of ghastliness and seems to sound a warning against his too absolute spirit, which is so inclined to "seeing nought, nought hearing" save itself.

To Wordsworth such absoluteness of spirit, or idealism—the *experience*, not the idea, of the mind as all-in-all—was a dangerous abyss. In the well-known note he dictated late in life about the *Immortality Ode*, he described his sense as a boy of "the indomitableness of the spirit within me": how external things did not exist independently for him but seemed to owe their existence to his thinking them. To recall himself "from this abyss of idealism to the reality," to *balance* himself against it, he would catch at a wall or a tree on his way to school.[11] This is so different from Coleridge. For the undejected Coleridge idealism was no abyss but the principle and power of self by which an inanimate, cold Nature was made to spring to life, by which he

> shot his being through earth, sea, and air,
> Possessing all things with intensest love.

(*France: An Ode*)

For the dejected Coleridge, however, the experience of idealism was also an abyss, but the abyss of Hamletism. Intellec-
tually, Coleridge knew that the answer to Hamlet subjectivity
was a perfected idealism, a refined realism: "true Idealism
necessarily perfecting itself in Realism, & Realism refining itself into Idealism."[12] Coleridge could think this answer, but
he couldn't live it. On the level of living he experienced his
idealism, ever more strongly, as a becoming shadowy and insubstantial, a tottering on the edge of nothing. Wordsworth's
feeling of an idealist supremacy of mind in himself was a feeling of overweening *strength*, of a mind and imagination threatening to overpower nature; Coleridge's was a feeling of weakness, of a failing hold on nature.

Coleridge talked all the time about the right relation between thoughts and things, and Wordsworth listened closely.
When he paid tribute to Coleridge at the end of *The Prelude* for
his part in shaping the growth of his mind, as we have seen,
he thanked his influence for the fact that "thoughts and
things / In the self-haunting spirit learned to take / More rational proportions." To Wordsworth, Coleridge's talking about
the "rational proportions" of thoughts and things was an
admonishment to correct the overbearing tendency of his
mind and imagination, recall it to this earth from the sublime
heights, chasten and restrain a dangerously exalted rapture.
It meant not to soar beyond human life, abandoning it. But to
Coleridge himself it meant not to fall out of human life, into a
limbo of abstracted mind. Coleridge indeed for his part, ad-
miring the masculine strength he didn't have, esteemed the
sublime Wordsworth far above the homely one: "I really consider it as a misfortune," he remarked in a letter in 1803, "that
Wordsworth ever deserted his former mountain Track to wan-
der in Lanes and allies." "The natural *tendency* of Wordsworth's mind," he wrote in the *Biographia*, "is to great objects
and elevated conceptions."[13]

Law and Impulse

Wordsworth's poetry is one long meditation on striving as against resting, militant doing as against quiet non-doing, strength as against mildness—the assertiveness (but also the tranquility) of mind as against the quiescence (but also the tumultuousness) of nature. The opposition of militancy and passiveness is always one between mind and nature; but now nature is assertive and mind passive, and now mind assertive and nature passive. The very first episodes of *The Prelude* are a loving study of this opposition as it was displayed in the "fierce, moody, patient, venturous, modest, shy" boy that Wordsworth had been. In these reminiscences of childhood exuberance, often touched with lawlessness (robbing somebody else's bird snares, plundering birds' nests, ice-skating on the river, making off with a skiff on a lakeshore) there is a moment of arrest or surprise in the boy's ordinary unreflective intentness on what he is doing, or an after-moment, and his consciousness suffers a sudden, shocking enlargement into self-consciousness: his mind, expanding (like a great body of water suddenly revealed) into self-reflection, embraces the busy boy who is himself and the scene around him in the active circle of its stillness.

One such reminiscence, for which Wordsworth never found a place in *The Prelude*, describes an expedition to the woods he made one day to gather nuts—though "gather" is too tame a word to suit the violent action that explodes in *Nutting*. Dressed against thorns and brambles in a man's old clothes, a huge knapsack over his shoulder and a tall nutting crook in his hand, the small child marching off full of "the eagerness of boyish hope" cuts a grotesque figure ("Figure quaint"); and slightly grotesque, too, in the familiar Wordsworth way, is the big Miltonic style of the blank verse in which the poet tells his little anecdote. After "forcing" his way over pathless rocks and through beds of matted fern and tangled

thickets (a baby Satan crossing Chaos to wreck Paradise), the
boy comes to an unspoiled nook where

> the hazels rose
> Tall and erect, with tempting clusters hung,
> A virgin scene!

Wordsworth, commenting on the poem in old age, said he
had been an "impassioned nutter"; in his passion the nutter
eyes this "banquet" with "wise restraint Voluptuous," holding back and lingering out his pleasure for twenty-three slow
lines—till abruptly

> up I rose,
> And dragged to earth both branch and bough, with crash
> And merciless ravage; and the shady nook
> Of hazels, and the green and mossy bower,
> Deformed and sullied, patiently gave up
> Their quiet being: and, unless I now
> Confound my present feelings with the past,
> Ere from the mutilated bower I turned
> Exulting, rich beyond the wealth of kings,
> I felt a sense of pain when I beheld
> The silent trees, and saw the intruding sky.

The pain the boy feels is the pain of awakening to a consciousness of the "quiet being" of nature he has violated,
which is at the same time an awakening to his own being vis-
à-vis nature's. The shock of awareness he suffers under "the
silent trees" and "the intruding sky" is also a shock of self-
awareness. Having been shocked into self-consciousness out
of the unselfconsciousness of animal appetite, the boy is
given pause. He will go out nutting again, but inevitably his
passion will diminish. Henceforth he must practice not a "voluptuous restraint" which feeds the appetite, but a restraint
which tames it down and changes it into quiet sympathy with
living nature: use nature with a "gentle hand," say the last
lines of the poem in admonishment, "for there is a spirit in

the woods." What *Nutting* describes is an experience in which the boy's appetitive and masterful relation to nature—his biological militancy—is beginning that evolution by which it is chastened into the man's contemplative one.

Yet Wordsworth still loves the ardent boy he was, still loves fierceness, and maintains a precarious balance of feeling in the poem between wild, impulsive energy and reflective mildness. He hates power as it is practised in the world, but as the boy practises it, in innocent lust, he loves it. But because it is a power of nature turned against nature itself, Wordsworth must deplore it too, and the boy must learn to give it up. The boy Wordsworth learns to know the pain of moral life, but not through any sin or Fall. As a child of the eighteenth century, Wordsworth is a Miltonist, but as such a child he has no feeling whatsoever for sin or a Fall. He isn't even sure that as a boy he felt the "sense of pain" he remembers himself feeling; with his unfailing honesty, he says that he may be reading his present feelings back into the past. But he *is* sure that the boy came away from the mutilated bower "exulting," feeling himself "rich beyond the wealth of kings," and he exults with him over his conquest even as he deprecates it. The poem is at the same time a poem of conquest and of anti-conquest, ending in a moment of Wordsworthian heart constriction when the triumphant boy and the glaring sky stand eye to eye in the violated grove.

The modern artist's portrait of himself as a young boy is of a delicate spirit shrinking back from the coarse vigor of his fellows. Stephen Dedalus feels "small and weak" on the playground of Clongowes Wood College and shrinks back in the football game from "the rude feet" of the others. But in Wordsworth's picture of himself as a boy, his feet are the rude ones. He "herded" with his fellows rather than shrinking from them; his boast is that he belonged to "a race of real children," which is to say children who were

> not too wise,
> Too learned, or too good, but wanton, fresh,
> And bandied up and down by love and hate;
> Fierce, moody, patient, venturous, modest, shy,
> Mad at their sports like withered leaves in winds.

He utters a prayer for these children:

> May books and Nature be their early joy
> And knowledge, rightly honoured with that name—
> Knowledge not purchased with the loss of power!
>
> (*Prel.* V, 436)

His program for real children is "books and Nature," reading and doing, knowledge and power. But Wordsworth is afraid that books betray nature, that the price of knowledge is the loss of vital power—that "knowledge," in the words of Yeats, "increases unreality." His fear is that "real children," as they grow up into knowledge and mental life, lose their real being.

Wordsworth had no smack of Hamlet; no man was more opposite, psychologically, to the Hamlet type; and yet he was afraid of the antagonism between mind and life. For this was something that extended beyond individual psychological disposition into the foundations of modern being. He was afraid that having to take thought tamed the pride and power of life. *Some* kind of loss there had to be. Remembering in Book II of *The Prelude* the tumultuous, outpouring vitality of his boyhood and early youth, he is moved to ask:

> Ah, is there one who ever has been young
> And needs a monitory voice to tame
> The pride of virtue and of intellect?
> And is there one, the wisest and the best
> Of all mankind, who does not sometimes wish

For things which cannot be, who would not give,
If so he might, to duty and to truth
The eagerness of infantine desire?

(II, 19)

If we remember the plenitude of being, of nature, that we enjoyed unselfconsciously in youth, is there the slightest danger of our overrating virtue and intellect, which are the wisdom of age? And is there anybody at all, even the best and wisest man alive, who doesn't sometimes wish that the powerful driving forces of our primitive infantine nature, our biological militancy, might be harnessed to the knowledge of what is required of us in manhood by duty and truth? But such a union belongs among the "things which cannot be."

Wordsworth in the great time of his powers loved a "madness" which was "like withered leaves in winds"; the word *wild* is honorific on his lips, though he most often uses it in oxymoronic conjunction with gentleness. In the lines he wrote about Coleridge's six-year-old son Hartley, he calls him "exquisitely wild," thus balancing exquisitely two opposites. Ten years later he describes his own infant daughter Catherine, in verse which has gone stiff (*Characteristics of a Child Three Years Old*), as "tractable, though wild." The wheeling, fluttering, plunging birds in *Home at Grasmere* have a kind of stillness about them; theirs is a "calm revelry." *Tintern Abbey* is, among other things, an elegiacal meditation on the loss of "aching joys" and "dizzy raptures." The poem begins in the midst of nature's wildness: in "a wild secluded scene," in a "wild green landscape" in which the hedgerows are "little lines of sportive wood run wild." The youth he remembers himself as being was as wild as the landscape through which he bounded. But that time is past; and by way of recompense for the loss of wild joy, he has come to feel the quiet joy which springs from "elevated thoughts," from a sublime sense of something which unites the world of nature and the mind of man; a motion and a spirit which animates and impels, equally, all thinking creatures and all the things in the world they think about. In the last paragraph of the poem, coming around to his beginning, Wordsworth recovers, but only vicariously, his former dizzy raptures "in the shooting lights" of his sister's "wild eyes." He as it were cancels for "a little while" the loss of what he was, through participation in his sister's still "infantine" eagerness. It is only for a little while, because her "wild ecstasies" too must in turn be "matured" by time into "sober pleasure," quiet joy.

Tintern Abbey describes a Schilleresque passage from *being* nature, in simple unselfconsciousness, to *seeking* it in thought and meditation. Wordsworth's personal history here expresses the emotional history of our civilization, the history of the modern unhappiness with civilization: there has been a loss of vital inner force, of instinctual eagerness and power, of natural being (being in nature), even though there has been a huge gain in intellectual and material power. He believes that his recompense for the loss of the unthinking joys of simple being is "abundant"; his attitude is that things balance out— he is a poet of consolations, not repinings. Yet the poem ends with the thought of his own death.

Wordsworth's exalted sense of a motion and a spirit that animates and drives, at once, the thinking mind and the objects of its thought, was an intuition of what Coleridge called the "one Life"* of mind united with nature. In the *Prelude* passage quoted above, the union of "duty and truth" with "the eagerness of infantine desire" is another expression of the same thing—but as an idea rather than an intuition. As an *idea* such a union belongs among the "things which cannot be," especially as an idea that emphasizes the moral aspect of the mind's side of the union ("duty"). Wordsworth was no sentimentalist about how human beings really behaved. But as an *intuition* the union is vision and prophecy: a prophecy of

*"O! the one Life within us and abroad. . . ."—*Eolian Harp.*

that redemption by which the human being who has been divided from his nature by the thinking mind of civilization will at last rejoin nature with his thinking mind in new unity of being. Wordsworth was no D. H. Lawrence throwing himself back into the arms of the old stone gods.* As a "Prophet of Nature" he looked forward into the the future—far forward, because he feared rather than hoped for the immediate future. Even though the age in which he lives be too weak to tread the ways of truth, he declares at the end of *The Prelude*, and

> fall back to old idolatry,
> Though men return to servitude as fast
> As the tide ebbs, to ignominy and shame
> By nations sink together,† we shall still
> Find solace in the knowledge which we have,
> Blest with true happiness if we may be
> United helpers forward of a day
> Of firmer trust, joint labourers in the work
> .   .   .   .
> Of their redemption, surely yet to come.
> Prophets of Nature, we to them will speak
> A lasting inspiration.

(XIII, 432)

Wordsworth was a paradoxicalist who didn't really care for paradoxes. They didn't have the look of truth. Truth is what he cared about, and his idea of truth was of something literal, simple, unexceptional, not startling or surprising.‡ Coleridge

---

*Though D. H. Lawrence was a Wordsworthian.

†I am reminded of a line—and more than a line—in Wilfred Owen's great poem *Strange Meeting*: "though nations trek from progress." World War I was a consummation of the Napoleonic ignominy and shame into which Wordsworth saw men by nations sinking together.

‡"Literalness is the necessary preface to his genius. Everything, for him, was what it was, and it was not anything else: the thing done or suffered, the thing seen or heard or read, touched him because it was so. In its being so he saw it as somehow self-guaranteeing—this was the heart of his naturalistic optimism. . . ."—John Jones, *The Egotistical Sublime* (1960), 15.

in an epigram calls Donne's poetry "fancy's maze and clue, /
Wit's forge and fire-blast, meaning's press and screw." That is
just the kind of thing Wordsworth didn't like—all that straining wit, all that forcing of the mind (all that *mind*!). When I call
the Wordsworth paradoxicalness Militant Quietism, I press
his meaning into too sharp an antithesis; I don't think he
would have cared for it. He wants his paradox to be a thing
(that first word in the Wordsworth philosophical vocabulary)
in the world with the irregular edges of things, unobtrusive
and unremarkable, not a sharply defined, glittering construc-
tion of the mind.* He felt that way in spite of the fact—
because of the fact—that, once he had been awakened into
self-consciousness, his sense of things was dominated by the
duality of himself-here-considering and the-world-over-there-
that-he-considers. In visionary moments the two—contemplator and contemplated, mind and nature—melted together.
But those moments came only occasionally, and meanwhile
Wordsworth tried to soften and accommodate the opposition
in a spirit of Wordsworthian benignity. Sometimes he is *too*
benign:

> From Nature doth emotion come, and moods of
> Calmness equally are Nature's gift:
> This is her glory—these two attributes
> Are sister horns that constitute her strength;
> This twofold influence is the sun and shower

---

*He criticized Byron's once-famous stanza about solitude in the midst of the
crowd (*Child Harold* II, XXVI) for being too epigrammatically worked up:
"The sentiment by being expressed in an *antithetical* manner, is taken out of
the Region of high and imaginative feeling, to be placed in that of point and
epigram. To illustrate my meaning . . . I refer to my own Lines on the Wye,
where you will find the same sentiment not formally put . . . but ejaculated
as it were fortuitously in the musical succession of preconceived feeling.
Compare the paragraph ending 'How often has my spirit turned to thee' and
the one where occur the lines
> And greeting where no kindness is and all
> The dreary intercourse of daily life,
with the lines of Lord Byron—and you will perceive the difference."—To R. P.
Gillies, June 9, 1817.

Of all her bounties, both in origin
And end alike benignant. Hence it is
That genius, which exists by interchange
Of peace and excitation, finds in her
His best and purest friend—from her receives
That energy by which he seeks the truth,
Is rouzed, aspires, grasps, struggles, wishes, craves
From her that happy stillness of the mind
Which fits him to receive it when unsought.

(Prel. XII, 1)

This is very cozy—peace and excitation skipping arm in arm
like schoolgirls, without a hint of trouble. How often Wordsworth's own moods of arousal and quiescence took the problematic forms of a restless excitement which exhausted and
distressed him, and a depressing melancholy. When he describes poetry in the Preface to the *Lyrical Ballads* as the product of an interaction between turbulent feelings and quiet reflection, he isn't complacent about the antithesis; he treats the
matter as complex and difficult. He doesn't emphasize the jar
of antithesis, but neither does he make antithesis innocuous.
It is there unobtrusively.

It is there unobtrusively (I choose examples almost at ran-
dom) in the lines expressing the gratitude he felt at the grave
of Robert Burns because the Scottish poet

showed my youth
How verse may build a princely throne
On humble truth.

A quiet antitheticalness pervades the passage at the beginning of Book VI of *The Prelude* (1850) about his going back
to Cambridge at the end of the summer vacation, when the
leaves were fading on the banks of Esthwaite Water:

I turned my face
Without repining from the coves and heights
Clothed in the sunshine of the withering fern;

Quitted, not loth, the mild magnificence
Of calmer lakes and louder streams.

The *withering* fern makes a kind of *sunshine*, he says in a line
that can't be admired too much; the *calmer* lakes and *louder*
streams unite into a *mild magnificence*. Here, for a moment,
there seems no limit to the power of Wordsworthian poetry,
when exercised on the natural world, to heal the division of
things.

An unobtrusive paradoxicalness is the substance of one of
Wordsworth's greatest lyric poems, a poem in which he ex-
pands the antithesis of energy and rest to its fullest scope and
thereby raises song into philosophy without sacrificing one
jot of song. Three years, the poet quietly begins, Lucy grew in
sun and shower; then Nature, saying no lovelier flower was
ever sown on earth, claims the child as hers and promises to
make a lady of her own. Nature goes on in the next stanza:

"Myself will to my darling be
Both law and impulse; and with me
The Girl, in rock and plain,
In earth and heaven, in glade, and bower,
Shall feel an overseeing power
To kindle or restrain."

This poem is about the power of nature, and Nature here in
the second stanza declares what her power is: it is the power
to be both law and impulse, to kindle biologically and restrain
morally—though *biologically* and *morally* emphasize crudely
the discursive note of distinction and definition sounded in
the phrase *law and impulse*. The distinction is there, yet not
defined so absolutely as to make nature's power to unify the
vital and the moral seem an impossible union, a paradoxical
ideal conception, and not a thing in the world.

Nature is the universe of sense. In claiming to be all in all to
Lucy—the thinking life of law and principle, as well as the living life of impulse and desire—she is claiming that the uni-

verse of sense experience is all.* Wordsworth, in the heyday
of his nature religion, makes that claim over and over. Sometimes he does it quietly by implication and sometimes by
ecstatic pronouncement, as in the peroration of *Home at Grasmere* ("Prospectus"), when he proclaims the perfect match of
mind and world:

> How exquisitely the individual Mind
>
> .   .   .   .
>
>   to the external World
> Is fitted:—and how exquisitely, too—
>
> .   .   .   .
>
> The external World is fitted to the Mind;
> And the creation (by no lower name
> Can it be called) which they with blended might
> Accomplish.
>
> (816)

Mind and world cohabit by the ordinary necessity of things,
together making up nature or the all. But when mind *marries*
nature in *knowing* love and holy passion, the blended might of
both creates a Perfected Nature, or Paradise. In that Paradise
Lucy is raised.

Nature, then, is a kind of religious, or transcendental, em-
piricist (in M. H. Abrams' words, a "natural supernatural-
ist"). In the specific realm of moral philosophy, she is claiming to resolve the conflict between duty (law) and desire
(impulse). However, to speak about "a conflict between duty
and desire" means to speak about a conflict between the inclinations of *sense* and a principle or law of conduct *not* drawn
from sense but from some other, nonempirical source. As
Kant says, our sensory impulses drive us toward this and that
satisfaction, pleasure, happiness; but there is nothing in the
push and pull of sense to account for our being *obliged* to do

---

*Wordsworth calls Grasmere "This all in all of nature" in an early version of
Home at Grasmere—PWW V, 318, app. crit.

or not do something. Kantian obligation requires us to do our duty in spite of sense, in spite of pleasure, in spite of happiness—*in spite of nature*. Kantian duty rests on the freedom to go against the necessity of (our) nature, to transcend the realm of sense impulses, where the laws of cause and effect rule by iron compulsion.

Something of this sense of going against nature must always stick to the idea of duty. Empirical moral philosophers don't talk about the conflict of duty with desire, law with impulse, but about "desire-frustration" and "desire-satisfaction." They stay inside the realm of sense experience, and staying there they have little use for the word *duty*. In our own empirical times the idea of duty has little meaning. When a moralist who claims he gets his sense of obligation from some place outside of experience uses the word *duty*, the empirical moralist will interpret the word to discover the desires concealed in it. For the latter, morality is an adjustment or harmonization of desires. John Stuart Mill describes the theory of life on which he based his "Utility, or Greatest Happiness Principle" of morality, as follows: "namely, that pleasure and freedom from pain are the only things desirable as ends; and that all desirable things . . . are desirable either for the pleasure inherent in themselves, or as a means to the promotion of pleasure and the prevention of pain."

Now when Wordsworth speaks about a restraining law set over against a kindling impulse, he expresses the idea of duty. But, paradoxically, he expresses the idea of duty in order to overcome it—not overcome it logically as a naturalistic philosopher by proving it false, null, nothing, but overcome it as a thing only too real, as the devouring lion of morality which is at last made to lie down with the lamb of being, the "ought" with the "is." Wordsworth is not an empirical moralist who offers a nature morality in place of the nonnatural moralities derived from God or reason; he is a natural-supernaturalist who would lead us out of morality entirely, into a paradisal

Nature. He is a man looking for salvation and he thinks—sometimes—that he has found it. He thinks this only sometimes because he is not a wild enthusiast—or not only a wild enthusiast—but also a hard-headed Englishman who must take into account his doubts as well as his hopes.

But to return to the poem, the stanzas that follow the two introductory ones concretely spell out Nature's program of tutelage, which is Lucy's history; they are a closely woven tissue of antitheses whose opposing terms are accommodated to each other in an ambience of supernal benignity. The girl shall be as sportive as the fawn, and also as silent and as calm as mute insensate things; as stately as the floating clouds, and as bending as the willow; and even in the most violent, discordant motions of the storm she shall discover a silent, sympathetic, shaping harmony:

> "She shall be sportive as the fawn
> That wild with glee across the lawn
> Or up the mountain springs;
> And hers shall be the breathing balm,
> And hers the silence and the calm
> Of mute insensate things.
>
> "The floating clouds their state shall lend
> To her; for her the willow bend;*
> Nor shall she fail to see
> Even in the motions of the Storm
> Grace that shall mould the Maiden's form
> By silent sympathy."

Then the incredible fifth stanza rises-sinks to a negative crescendo of passionate quiescence, the Wordsworth solitude in which Lucy lives turning into a state of outright magic:

> "The stars of midnight shall be dear
> To her; and she shall lean her ear

---

*The willow bends in deference to her "state," as well as to teach her to bend. Lucy has state, has freedom, and she *commands* as well as being commanded.

In many a secret place
Where rivulets dance their wayward round,
And beauty born of murmuring sound
Shall pass into her face."

The next-to-last stanza turns again to the girl's "stateliness":

"And vital feelings of delight
Shall rear her form to stately height,
Her virgin bosom swell;
Such thoughts to Lucy I will give
While she and I together live
Here in this happy dell."

For the first time Nature speaks of Lucy's "thoughts"; Lucy is not after all a fawn, a cloud, a willow. Here for a moment an obscurity passes across the absolutely clear face of the poem. *Such thoughts* refers back, but to what? It must be to Lucy's "vital feelings of delight," and after that to all the exuberant-quiet feelings Nature has planned for her in the previous stanzas; for nothing that we normally call thoughts is attributed to Lucy in the poem. Feelings are thoughts, thoughts feelings.

Nature had promised in the second stanza that she would oversee Lucy as a restraining power as well as a kindling one. However, she is severer in word than in deed; the restraint exercised over Lucy, as it is shown in the poem, is not so much a blocking or interdiction of desires as a conducting and leading of them into quiet channels. The restraint of duty has been tempered and softened to the mildest kind of control. Turbulence and quiet, command and submission, spontaneity and thoughtfulness all seem, in the poem, satisfied nature. The Kantian defeat of desires and the Millian satisfaction of them, together, make up the paradox of a Perfected Nature.

But in the last stanza, Nature's work only just begun, Lucy

dies. Maybe the union of law and impulse cannot be; maybe it can exist only as

> The memory of what has been,
> And never more will be.

Three Years She Grew in Sun and Shower is an elegy which expresses a lover's regret; it is also, equally, an expression of philosophical regret. Wordsworth expresses that regret often in his poetry; it is the Wordsworthian regret. "Fair seed-time had my soul, and I grew up / Fostered alike by beauty and by fear," Book I of *The Prelude* announces by way of introduction to the anecdotes of boyhood escapades. These are also philosophical anecdotes. The beauty and the fear that fostered the boy are the kindling and restraining powers, impulse and law, by which Nature fostered Lucy, who dies. The boy Wordsworth also dies, dies into thought. He ceases to *be* nature in "Delight and Liberty, the simple creed / Of Childhood," but by way of compensation becomes her worshiper, takes comfort from the philosophic mind that the years bring him— from the thoughts, often reaching to a depth of enduring being below all human vicissitudes, that the meanest flower inspires in him. At the conclusion of the painful *Ruined Cottage*, the sight of that ruin's high-grown weeds and grass, silvered by the mist and silent raindrops, conveys "so still an image of tranquility" to the poet's mind, which is agitated by the spectacle of human suffering, that, he writes:

> what we feel of sorrow and despair
> From ruin and from change, and all the grief
> The passing shews of being leave behind,
> Appeared an idle dream that could not live
> Where meditation was. I turned away,
> And walked along my road in happiness.

There is the being which is a passing show, with all its suffering and sorrow. But meditation reaches, Hamlet-like, to "that within which passeth show." Only Wordsworthian meditation, turning *Hamlet* upside down, discovers happiness deep inside itself, not woe.

Human and Sublime

When Wordsworth got his degree in 1791 he was not eager to take up a profession in the world. Poetry was not a profession, and anyhow it would be some years before he felt he could call himself a poet. He hated the idea of going into the church, which was the most likely fate awaiting him, or into the law. If he could have his own way—which in fact he did have, which he always had—he preferred postponing any decision about an occupation and doing nothing; and he postponed things so well that by the middle of the decade, thanks to a legacy left him by an admirer, he was in the position of being able to scrape by as an "idle" poet, without an occupation. * But in his old age he confessed that there was one profession he had wished to follow in his youth, the profession of arms. "He had read books of military history and strategy, and thought he had 'a talent for command.'" Mrs. Moorman goes on to say that his

> desire for a military career is not so surprising as at first appears. His fundamental patriotism, bred from his reading of history and heroic legend, † was as yet undisturbed by the French Revolution. That the disturbance was only temporary is shown by his deep concern for national defence and his joining the volunteers

*De Quincey is funny in his *Recollections* about what he thought was Wordsworth's exasperatingly good luck in life, his "God-sends" of money falling into his lap just when they were needed and enabling him to go on doing as he pleased. "A more fortunate man," he wrote, "does not exist than Wordsworth." Raisley Calvert's bequest was the first such godsend.

†   Land of our fathers! precious unto me
    Since the first joy of thinking infancy;
    When of thy gallant chivalry I read,
    And hugged the volumes on my sleepless bed!

                                    (PWW III, 159, app. crit.)

after the resumption of the war with France in 1803, and by his detestation of Bonaparte. Wordsworth was the author of *Poems dedicated to National Independence and Liberty* as well as of *Lyrical Ballads*. He loved the soldierly virtues.[14]

The soldierly bent in Wordsworth expressed the disposition of his character toward sternness and severity, energy and power—toward the militant and sublime rather than the domestic. There was always in him, he says in *The Prelude*,

> something of stern mood, an under-thirst
> Of vigour, never utterly asleep.
>
> (VI, 489)

This stern and vigorous mood, he writes at the very end of the poem by way of summing up, was his natural and fundamental one and dominated in him till his late twenties. It was the reason why he

> Too exclusively esteemed that love,
> And sought that beauty, which as Milton sings
> Hath terror in it.
>
> (XIII, 224)

Wordsworth was naturally inclined to the sublime, to the grand and elevated forms of love that move one with fear and awe, to the kind of beauty that is edged with terror; and he was naturally disinclined to the commonplace. But militancy and sublimity tend toward the inhuman, and he had learned to be afraid of losing touch with human life. Wordsworth felt the danger of inhumanness on one side, banality on the other. Against the latter danger he was fully armed in himself as a lover of solitude, meditation, and poetry. Against the former danger there always stood his sister, she who gave him eyes and gave him ears,

> And humble cares, and delicate fears;
> A heart, the fountain of sweet tears;
>   And love, and thought, and joy.
>
> (*Sparrow's Nest*)

Thanks to Dorothy his rigorous, soldierlike character was mollified and humanized:

> Thou didst soften down
> This over-sternness; but for thee, sweet friend,
> My soul, too reckless of mild grace, had been
> Far longer what by Nature it was framed—
> Longer retained its countenance severe—
> A rock with torrents roaring, with the clouds
> Familiar, and a favorite of the stars;
> But thou didst plant its crevices with flowers,
> Hang it with shrubs. . . .
>
> (*Prel.* XIII, 226)

After Dorothy it is Coleridge whom he thanks for helping to humanize a nature too Alp-like and at home among the clouds and stars. Even though Coleridge taught him most of the philosophy he ever learned—as he ever cared to learn, after his revolutionary days*—he thanks his influence, not as you would expect for encouraging his mind to mount to visionary heights, but on the contrary for "chastening" and damping down its overreadiness to flights of metaphysical rapture, to living a perpetual ontological hallelujah.† And though we connect Coleridge's name first of all with the idea

---

*In the Preface to the *Lyrical Ballads* Wordsworth writes, with amusing lack of pretension to even a little philosophical reading: "Aristotle, *I have been told*, has said that Poetry is the most philosophical of all writing: it is so . . ." (emphasis mine). (Aristotle doesn't say this; what he says is that poetry is more philosophical than history. The one who must have told Wordsworth this is Coleridge. Years later we find Coleridge making just such an interpretation of the famous passage in the *Poetics*, in Chap. 22 of the *Biographia Literaria*. There, ironically enough, he is quoting the passage against Wordsworth, whose tendency to overcircumstantiality ["accidentality"] he criticizes as an offense against the essential generality of poetry [see PrW I, 79]).

† And so the deep enthusiastic joy,
   The rapture of the hallelujah
   Sent from all that breathes and is, was chastened, stemmed,
   And balanced, by a reason which indeed
   Is reason, duty, and pathetic truth.
   (*Prel.* XIII, 261)

of the great unity of things, Wordsworth is grateful to him for
helping him to think less rather than more about "the one Life
within us and abroad." Thanks to Coleridge's "gentle spirit,"
Wordsworth's ecstatic poring on the life

> Of all things and the mighty unity
> In all which we behold, and feel, and are,

relaxed in its fierce concentration and made room for thoughts

> Of man and his concerns, such as become
> A human creature, be he who he may,
> Poet, or destined to an humbler name.

(Prel. XIII, 254)

The strong bent of Wordsworth's character to the militant-
sublime had its psychological origins in his personality; his
mistrust of that bent arose out of his personal culture. Because Wordsworth was a solid—that is, materialist (Baconian-
Miltonian-Newtonian)—Englishman, impatient of all philosophical ideas except his own (which as his own he treats as
natural sentiments rather than ideas), his mind was naturalistic, empirical. He admired the sublime above all as being supremely poetical, but its tendency to fly off the face of the
earth into spheres beyond the natural* made him uneasy. As
an enthusiast of revolution he had done just that—flown off
the face of the earth in pursuit of sublime visions of new
worlds. The overweening, unawed, upstart[†] rationality he
had been led into as a revolutionary had brought him to the
brink of breakdown by cutting him off from the wellsprings of

---

*"The natural" being for him essentially all the sensations and experiences of
the world he grew up in as a boy and to which he returned as a poet: Cockermouth and Hawkshead and Grasmere.

[†]In the 1850 *Prelude* Burke is described as standing on the floor of Parliament
"like an oak whose stag-horn branches start / Out of its leafy brow" and ridi-
culing "all systems built on abstract rights":
> the majesty proclaims
> Of Institutes and Laws, hallowed by time;
> Declares the vital power of social ties

his life. Wordsworth's religious intuitions were always heterodox, but the moral suspicion that he ever afterwards harbored toward his own unruly, restless temper conformed to old religious tradition. He must be "lowly wise" and think only about what concerned him and his being, not "dream of other worlds."

An activist and militant in his impulses, in the moral disposition of his mind he was a quietist counselling men to keep their place as quiet creatures of the earth; so the vocation of sublimity made him nervous. By its very exaltation it raised him far above the ordinary cares and concerns of suffering humanity and the common life out of which love and tenderness are born, into a deathly region of unrelieved spirituality. In a fragmentary essay entitled "The Sublime and the Beautiful," he writes that "though it is impossible that a mind can be in a healthy state that is not frequently and strongly moved both by sublimity and beauty, it is more dependent for its daily well-being upon the love & gentleness which accompany the one, than upon the exaltation or awe which are created by the other." [15] Wordsworth is saying the mind needs to experience both sublimity and beauty for its health, and we recollect the lines in *The Prelude*:

> Fair seed-time had my soul, and I grew up
> Fostered alike by beauty and by fear.
>
> (I, 305)

But for its daily well-being, for its *living* life, the mind needs the human love and gentleness which accompany beauty more than it needs the superhuman of the sublime. You feel his fear lurking inside his thought (a familiar enough fear in later times) that sublimity is not connected with the health of the

---

Endeared by Custom; and with high disdain,
Exploding upstart Theory, insists
Upon the allegiance to which men are born.

(VII, 520)

mind at all but with its morbidity, its Hamletism—that is, with power of mind that estranges you from life. *

This same ambiguous attitude toward the sublime is betrayed in the distinction Wordsworth draws between a "poetical" and a "human" imagination, in the preface to his *Poems* of 1815:

> The grand storehouses of enthusiastic and meditative Imagination, of poetical, as contra-distinguished from human and dramatic Imagination, are the prophetic and lyrical parts of the Holy Scriptures, and the works of Milton; to which I cannot forbear to add those of Spenser. I select these writers in preference to those of ancient Greece and Rome, because the anthropomorphitism of the Pagan religion subjected the minds of the greatest poets in those countries too much to the bondage of definite form; from which the Hebrews were preserved by their abhorrence of idolatry. This abhorrence was almost as strong in our great epic Poet, both from circumstances of his life, and from the constitution of his mind. However imbued the surface might be with classical literature, he was a Hebrew in his soul; and all things tended in him toward the sublime. . . . Of the human and dramatic Imagination the works of Shakespeare are an inexhaustible source.

There is an "enthusiastic and meditative Imagination," which is "poetical," and there is a "human and dramatic Imagination": the poetical or sublime imagination (the Hebrew prophets', Milton's, Spenser's—and his own) is not human; and the human imagination (Shakespeare's), it would seem, is not poetical.

The editors of Wordsworth's prose works tell us the distinction is not his but that of John Dennis, the neo-Longinian critic who early in the eighteenth century championed feel-

---

* "When I ventured to express my regret at Sir Joshua Reynolds giving so much of his time to portrait painting and to his Friends, I did not mean to recommend absolute solitude and seclusion from the world as an advantage to him or anybody else. I think it a great evil; and indeed in the case of a Painter, frequent intercourse with the living world seems absolutely necessary to keep the mind in health and vigour."—To Sir George Beaumont, Aug. 31, 1804.

ing and especially the sublime feelings. Dennis divided the "passions" into "Vulgar" or "ordinary," and "Enthusiastick": "Vulgar Passion . . . is that which is moved by the Objects themselves, or by the Ideas in the ordinary Course of Life . . . Enthusiastick Passion, or Enthusiasm, is a Passion which is moved by the Ideas in Contemplation, or the Meditation of things that belong not to common Life." [16] Dennis distinguishes the common life with its immediate impressions, feelings, and ideas—all of which, he says a few lines later, supply the stuff of drama—from the "enthusiastick" life of meditation on sublime things. Wordsworth takes over Dennis's distinction between the common life (of action) and the enthusiastic life (of thoughts) and radicalizes it into an opposition between the human and the poetical: for him what is essentially *poetical* is lofty meditation, abstracted soaring *thoughts*, and what is essentially human and dramatic is common, or immediate and unabstracted, life.

In the Essay Supplementary to the 1815 Preface, Wordsworth recurs to his opposition between the human and the poetical-meditative. Modifying and partly reconciling this opposition, he writes that there is "a meditative, as well as a human, pathos; an enthusiastic, as well as an ordinary, sorrow; a sadness that has its seat in the depths of the reason, to which the mind cannot sink gently of itself—but to which it must descend by treading the steps of thought." * Such a division

---

*This was no new idea for Wordsworth. It had been growing in him from as far back as 1797–98, for he says much the same thing in *The Ruined Cottage*, to explain what he is up to as a poet:

    The Poets, in their elegies and songs
    Lamenting the departed, call the groves,
    They call upon the hills and streams to mourn,
    And senseless rocks—nor idly, for they speak
    In these their invocations with a voice
    Obedient to the strong creative power
    Of human passion. Sympathies there are
    More tranquil, yet perhaps of kindred birth,
    That steal upon the meditative mind
    And grow with thought.

                                      (73)

of poetry and feeling bears an obvious relation to Schiller's division of poets into naive and sentimental: "The ancient [naive] poets move us by their truth of nature, truth of sense, by their living immediacy; the modern [sentimental] poets move us by ideas." Of course, the division doesn't belong to this man or that man but to an age, an age in which the poet's self, in realizing itself by separation from the world, realizes, in exultation and dismay, that it is separated from the world.

Because Wordsworth locates the essence of the poetical in sublime meditations, it is not surprising that for him there is an affinity (as he says in the Essay Supplementary) "between religion—whose element is infinitude, and whose ultimate trust is the supreme of things, submitting herself to circumscription, and reconciled to substitutions; and poetry—ethereal and transcendent, yet incapable to sustain her existence without sensuous incarnation." That is his boast and his fear. With such ideas as these about the nature of poetry, Wordsworth finds himself in an embarrassing position with respect to Shakespeare, the position of saying that Shakespeare's poetry is not as "poetical" as his own. (Charles Lamb felt that Wordsworth was not embarrassed enough!) The faithful reporter Crabb Robinson tells us that while he was out walking with Wordsworth in 1812, the latter "talked much of poetry and with great and, to me, laudable freedom of his own poems. He said that perhaps there is as *intense* poetical feeling in *his* as Shakespeare's works, but in Shakespeare the poetical elements are mixed up with other things and wrought into greater works. In him the poetry is *reiner* [purer]." [17] By "laudable freedom" Robinson means Wordsworth's saying so openly that he thought himself the purer poet, even though Shakespeare was the greater.

In light of this remark, one understands better the reach of Wordsworth's sentence about a "sighing" Shakespeare in the Essay Supplementary: "Grand thoughts (and Shakespeare must often have sighed over this truth), as they are most naturally and most fitly conceived in solitude, so can they not be brought forth in the midst of plaudits, without some violation of their sanctity." He doesn't only mean that Shakespeare had to please the pit. He means the whole audience is a pit, the stage a pit, the common life of men a pit; that as a "human and dramatic" poet Shakespeare was dragged down from the heights of the transcendent and compelled to be less pure than the solitary poet meditating his far-ranging thoughts. Wordsworth admired *Hamlet* extremely. "There is more mind in *Hamlet*," he said in conversation, "than in any other play, more knowledge of human nature." [18] But as he didn't admire plays in general, because the stage was inhospitable to mind, there is perhaps some qualification in his finding more mind in *Hamlet* than in any other *play*. *

The romantic (and modern) sense of spirit as a lurking rather than a manifest thing, as something that is shy of public appearances, that fades at cockcrow, preferred Shakespeare in the mind, as a vision, to Shakespeare on the stage as a representation. It liked reading him better than seeing him. Shakespeare acted was always a disappointment, Hazlitt thought ("A View of the Stage"). Goethe said there was much less *sinnliche That* (physical action) than *geistiges Wort* (expression of thought) in Shakespeare's plays, and therefore they were better read than seen. Lamb wrote about the tragedies ("Considered with Reference to Their Fitness for Stage Representation") that in viewing them on the stage "we have only materialized and brought down a fine vision to the standard of flesh and blood. We have let go a dream, in quest of an unattainable substance." But Wordsworth is more drastic, suggesting that there is in the nature of the theater itself an inherent repugnance to elevated ideas and that this was what made Shakespeare sigh. †

*He was not much of a playgoer. "I never saw Hamlet acted my self nor do I know what kind of play they make of it," he said at the age of thirty-five.—To Sir George Beaumont, May 1, 1805.

†"A dramatic Author, if he write for the stage, must adapt himself to taste of the audience, or they will not endure him."—Essay Suppl. Wordsworth im-

Though Lamb vindicated a more ethereal Shakespeare of the mind against a Shakespeare materialized on the stage, he did not extend this into a principle which included Wordsworth's ethereality, or at least the kind of ethereal narrative represented by Wordsworth's long narrative poem *The White Doe of Rylstone*. About that poem, it seems, Lamb complained (after hearing Wordsworth read an early draft of it) that the main characters didn't *do* anything, that it lacked "the common excitements of lively interest, namely, curiosity and the terror or pity from unusual external Events & Scenes." (We know Lamb's opinion only indirectly from an exchange of letters between Wordsworth and Coleridge in 1808.) Wordsworth's rebuttal of Lamb's criticism was vehement and insulting. He wrote Coleridge (April 19, 1808) that he knew Lamb could never like the poem; Wordsworth had told Lamb it could never be popular because the catastrophe was intellectual rather than material, the actions being events of the imagination in the characters' minds and therefore "fine-spun and inobtrusive." The charge that the chief characters do nothing was "false and too ridiculous."

> When it is considered what has already been executed in Poetry, strange that a man cannot perceive . . . that this is the time when a man of genius may honourably take a station upon different ground. If he is to be a Dramatist, let him crowd his scene with gross and visible action; but if a narrative Poet, if the Poet is to be predominant over the Dramatist,—then let him see if there are no victories in the world of spirit, no changes, no commotions, no revolutions there, no fluxes and refluxes of the thoughts which may be made interesting by modest combination with the stiller actions of the bodily frame, or with the gentler movements and milder appearances of society and social intercourse, or the still

---

plies that a dramatic poet who doesn't have to please an audience—who writes closet dramas—is free to think grand thoughts. He has in mind the author of *Samson Agonistes*. He said his own single venture into tragedy, *The Borderers*, had been written "without any view to its exhibition on the stage."—PWW I, 342.

more mild and gentle solicitations of irrational and inanimate nature.

But Lamb couldn't appreciate such poetry because he didn't have "a reasoning mind," nor therefore "a comprehensive mind, and, least of all, had he an imaginative one."*

In his letter to Coleridge, Wordsworth self-consciously takes his stand on different ground from that of the traditional Aristotelian idea of poetry and distinguishes, with some contempt, between drama with its gross and visible actions, and a narrative poetry of the mind acting imaginatively. Later on in the 1815 Preface and the Essay Supplementary to the

---

*Coleridge's opinion of *The White Doe* had been pretty much the same as Lamb's: he thought it suffered from "a disproportion of the Accidents to the spiritual Incidents," he wrote (bravely!) to Wordsworth. He had even figured out a way, by introducing some "little incidents" into the poem, to achieve a better balance of inner and outer. But then he quailed before Wordsworth's vehemence: "But after my receipt of your Letter concerning Lamb's censures I felt my courage fail—and that what I deemed a harmonizing would disgust you, as a *materialization* of the Plan [of the poem], & appear to you like insensibility to the power of the history in the mind."—CL III, 108.

"Disproportion of the Accidents to the spiritual Incidents" means lacking suitable "objective correlative." Coleridge and Wordsworth both express something like the idea contained in Eliot's phrase a century before Eliot. (I have already had occasion to touch on this—see p. 28.) They were not being especially original; the idea was in the air, a part of the romantic Zeitgeist, and it can look two ways. One way, as in Coleridge and Wordsworth, sees, Hamlet-fashion, how unable the outer life is to denote truly the spirit within. The other way, as in Eliot, sees the restoration of the classical harmony of inner and outer as depending on the reunion of the dissociated sensibility, ultimately on abandoning modern heresies and recovering religious truth.

Eliot, in middle age, said the popularity of the phrases *dissociation of sensibility* and *objective correlative* astonished him. They were such hits, I think, because of their scientific sound. The young Eliot used words like *facts* and *data* a lot; "Tradition and the Individual Talent" makes a famous chemical analogy. Eliot was a traditionalist, but a tough-minded, modernizing one. He despised the genteelly, narrowly literary. He wanted a criticism that was hard-nosed, exact, unafraid of judgment, not amateurish and appreciative; one that would crush contemptuously the soft and invertebrate, academic and popular Romanticism he found prevailing in the life and literature around him. That was why he was a classicist, because Classicism seemed hard-nosed and exact. But to classicize is itself purely romantic.

Preface, basing himself on Dennis, Wordsworth proposes this as a distinction between the human and dramatic imagination and the enthusiastic and meditative imagination. But the letter shows how he would like to deny that drama, gross and visible as it is, is truly imaginative. He isn't worrying, in an angry letter, about the implications of his view for Shakespeare; his mind is not on the problems of just criticism but on himself, on defending himself and his mission as a revolutionary poet. And this mission, as he conceives it, is to move poetry out of the gross and visible scene into the soul of man. His words signal the disappearance of story from poetry (and in the twentieth century from narrative and drama, too).

The notion of his being a purer, more poetical poet than Shakespeare didn't just occur to Wordsworth once in conversation. It is present in his thinking about the nature of poetry in the 1815 Preface and Essay Supplementary to the Preface, and something like it is present almost from the start of his career. Commenting in *The Ruined Cottage* on that poem's own story, he writes:

> 'Tis a common tale
> By moving accidents uncharactered,
> A tale of silent suffering, hardly clothed
> In bodily form, and to the grosser sense
> But ill adapted, scarcely palpable
> To him who does not think.
>
> (231)

Wordsworth, looking back on English poetry with his modern historical consciousness, created for himself ("half created and perceived") a line or tradition to which he self-consciously adhered, the line of Milton, Spenser, and the Hebrew Bible. And because he knew what he owed his predecessors, he knew what he owed to himself alone; he knew himself as an original poet who, he wrote in the Essay Supplementary, was "called upon to clear and often to shape his own road," like "Hannibal among the Alps."

Charles Lamb, writing to a friend earlier in that same year of 1808, on February 26th, had had occasion to exclaim as indignantly about Wordsworth as we have just seen Wordsworth exclaiming about him. That lover of Shakespeare, not as tolerant as Crabb Robinson, had been outraged by the modern poet's comparing himself to the elder one:

> Wordsworth [Lamb wrote] the great poet is coming to town. He is to have apartments in the Mansion House. He says he does not see much difficulty in writing like Shakespeare, if he had a mind to try it. It is clear that nothing is wanting but the mind.

Lamb's sardonic pun on mind ridicules his heavy friend's pretentions, his "hardihood of assertion" as he calls it in his letter. However, what looks like megalomania on Wordsworth's part is really a defiant assertion of himself as a great *modern* poet vis-à-vis the great elder poet Shakespeare, cast into the teeth of a shallow, indifferent public. Though Lamb mocks "the great poet" and visiting VIP, and though Wordsworth in his middle years was indeed a figure of some importance who might put up at the Mansion House, which was the official residence of the Lord Mayor, Wordsworth was nevertheless feeling unappreciated and angry. The two-volume edition of his lyrical poems that he published in 1807, collecting five years' work, had been roughly handled by the reviewers and had sold poorly. Wordsworth was attacked for doting perversely on low subjects, for making an incomprehensible fuss about trivial things. Meanwhile Scott was capturing the public taste, and in a few years' time Byron would take it by storm. Wordsworth's confidence and pride in himself as a poet were indomitable but never imperturbable. All his life he explained and defended (and corrected) his poems with painful earnestness ("sweated," as Lamb writes in another letter) in response to criticisms made by relatives, friends, friends of friends, and also critics, never mind who; he never simply smiled or was disdainful. And in fact as a critic of his own poems he is very good; his own comments remain among the most pertinent things said about them. But feeling more and more resentful in his middle years because of what he regarded as the critics' malicious lack of appreciation and the London world's shallow ignorance of all that he had done, with inurbane bluntness he asserted his own greatness as a poet, claimed for himself the "Vision and the Faculty divine."

Wordsworth, quoting Coleridge, wrote more than once that "every author, as far as he is great and at the same time *original*, has had the task of *creating* the taste by which he is to be enjoyed." The undignified implication of this in the realm of reputation is that every great and original author has himself to din it into others how great he is. When Wordsworth told Lamb he could write like Shakespeare if he wanted to, he was stubbornly insisting on the originality and worth of his own work, his own purposes: He could write in the way of Shakespeare if he had a mind to, but what *he* had in mind was to write in his own way, which is to say the way of the modern poet treading the steps of thought down into "the Mind of Man":

> Not Chaos, not
> The darkest pit of lowest Erebus,
> Nor aught of blinder vacancy, scooped out
> By help of dreams—can breed such fear and awe
> As fall upon us often when we look
> Into our Minds, into the Mind of Man—
> My haunt and the main region of my song.

Sublimity made Wordsworth uneasy; yet it was as a sublime poet that the middle-aged writer justified himself in 1815 (though his was a new kind of sublimity). True, his poetry wasn't popular. But what kind of test of excellence was popularity, he exclaimed in the Essay Supplementary:

> If we consider what are the cares that occupy the passing day, and how remote is the practice and the course of life from the sources of sublimity, in the soul of Man, can it be wondered that

there is little existing preparation [in the popular mind] for a
poet charged with a new mission to extend its kingdom and to
augment and spread its enjoyments?

By his "new mission" as a poet of modern sublimity Wordsworth meant the exercise of an imagination that was pecu-
liarly reflective, the "enthusiastic and meditative imagination"
of the self-conscious mind of modern times. He had some
precedents: the Hebrew prophets in antiquity and, in the English past, Milton; but in general the imagination and wisdom
of olden times were instinctive and passional rather than reflective and self-reflective. It belonged to his mission to unite
old and new:

> In everything which is to send the soul into herself, to be ad-
> monished of her weakness, or to be made conscious of her
> power;—wherever life and nature are described as operated
> upon by the creative or abstracting virtue of the imagination;
> wherever the instinctive wisdom of antiquity and her heroic
> passions uniting, in the heart of the poet, with the meditative
> wisdom of later ages, have produced that accord of sublimated
> humanity, which is at once a history of the remote past and a
> prophetic enunciation of the remotest future, *there*, the poet
> must reconcile himself for a season to few and scattered hearers.

His is a poetry of the *soul*, a poetry that is able to unite the
natural-heroic with the inward and the meditative so as to
bring about an *accord of sublimated humanity*, a reconciliation of
the historical past, stretching away behind, with the prophetic
future extending illimitably before—a poetry of first, and
last, and midst, and without end. Earlier in the Essay Supplementary Wordsworth says much the same thing when he
describes "the higher poetry"—*his* poetry—as combining
"the wisdom of the heart and the grandeur of the imagination": heart *and* imagination, earthly nature *and* sublime mind.
"Wherever these appear, simplicity accompanies them; Magnificence herself when legitimate, depending upon a simplic-

ity of her own, to regulate her ornaments." Magnificence-cum-simplicity is the stylistic formula for the union of mind and nature. As always, Wordsworth is a poet of reconciliations and reunions and is striving to have it both ways. But this is something by the way in 1815. For now Wordsworth's first concern, as a poet aggrieved by lack of public appreciation, is to stress the large side of his verse, the side of its "grandeur" and "magnificence."

All his life Wordsworth held an exalted conception of the poet's function. But the first comprehensive statement of his ideas about poetry, the 1800 Preface to the *Lyrical Ballads*, which justified his practice in that volume, stressed little poetry over big, simple over grand. He deliberately took, he said, his subjects from lowly rustic life, his language from the real language of men living in those circumstances. He "utterly rejected" personifications of abstract ideas, the "gaudiness and inane phraseology" of poetic diction (which was the degenerate offspring of the Miltonic Grand Style)—all "devices to elevate the style, and raise it above prose." What he aimed at was "to keep the Reader in the company of flesh and blood." Hardly ever does he apply the terms *divine* and *sublime* to poetry and poets, and when he does, they are no more than honorific. It is the humanness of poetry which Wordsworth is at pains to defend and uphold in his first Preface, not its superhumanness, its divinity: the poet "is the rock of defence for human nature."

In the 1800 Preface the imagination is a tame enough power and little dwelt on by the poet. It provides "a certain colouring . . . whereby ordinary things should be presented to the mind in an unusual aspect"; or it enables the poet to feel, more than others, "absent things as if they were present"; or to produce feelings in himself nearer to the feelings produced by real events than is the case with other men. The language which even the greatest poet's imagination suggests to him "must fall short of that which is uttered by men in real life";

the imitative effort of the poet "is in some degree mechanical, compared with the freedom and power of real and substantial action and suffering." Wordsworth's first account of the imagination subordinates it to "real life," whose power and simplicity it can only strive to emulate. As a mimetic power, auxiliary to nature, the imagination does nature's work where nature can't do it directly itself—that is, in "the works of man," to quote *The Prelude* (XIII, 181), the works of art and civilization. The reason why the imagination gets along so well with the real world is that "man and nature [are] essentially adapted to each other, and the mind of man [is] naturally the mirror of the fairest and most interesting properties of nature." The poetic mind belongs with nature and makes part of it; the poet "sings" like a bird.

Yet in the *Lyrical Ballads* is a poem which is hardly ballad or birdsong, the meditative *Tintern Abbey*. And appropriate to the presence of that poem in the volume is Wordsworth's touching on, but not stressing, the role of thought in poetic composition, thought which abstracts us from nature and sets us over against it. He writes, in his famous formula, that poetry, "all good poetry, is the spontaneous overflow of powerful feelings." But he quickly adds (what is so often forgotten) that the poet "must also have thought long and deeply" about his subject, in addition to feeling it powerfully. Out of the mind brooding dovelike over feeling comes poetic composition.

But fifteen years later, with his greatest works behind him— and especially that exploration of the imagination and its grandiose possibilities, *The Prelude*—a marked shift of emphasis in Wordsworth's ideas about poetry has taken place. The new emphasis is the result of what he has learned from his experience as a poet, abetted by his need to vindicate his greatness. Now he stresses the primacy of the imagination and its "almost divine powers." Now the divinity of poetry, the divinity of *his* poetry, concerns him more than its humanity. No longer is the imagination a "coloring" agent; now it is a power that "shapes and *creates*" (the emphasis is his). The word *create* was already commonly used in Wordsworth's day to characterize what poets and all great artists did, but it wasn't the commonplace term it is today. It still remembered its origins. Originally the verb *to create* had a highly restricted meaning. It meant what God did and nobody else: to create was to create the Creation. But then it began to mean a power men, too, could exercise. William Collins says exultingly in his *Ode on the Poetical Character* that the human imagination was born on the same day that God exercised his to make the world—"on that creating day," he rhapsodizes,

> When He called with thought to birth
> Yon tented sky, this laughing earth,
> And dresst [it] with springs, and forests tall,
> And pour'd the main engirting all.

To say that the imagination creates was to say that the poet possesses a power like God's. That power works by "innumerable processes" having their inception, Wordsworth writes, in "a sublime consciousness of the soul in her own mighty and almost divine powers."

How the imagination creates, by endowing objects with properties or abstracting them away, by modifying and moulding, by making the many one and the one many, Wordsworth describes in the 1815 Preface. That is his literary-practical account of the imagination. But he also gives a metaphysical account of it. The metaphysical function of the imagination is "to incite and to support the eternal": "Fancy is given to quicken and to beguile the temporal part of our nature, Imagination to incite and to support the eternal." As a power of mind exercised in the interest of the eternal part of our nature, to reveal it and sustain it, the imagination is essentially and intrinsically sublime: imaginative, that means sublime.

In Book II of *The Prelude* Wordsworth records how he liked to walk alone among his native hills in stormy weather or at night, listening to the winds or the nighttime sounds of earth. On such occasions, when the ear was open and the eye dimmed, he experienced a mood of exaltation in which, rising above the world of concrete, visible forms and images, he felt the imaginative power—imaginative power *in general*—passing into him as if he drank it:

> I would walk alone
> In storm or tempest, or in starlight nights
> Beneath the quiet heavens, and at that time
> Have felt whate'er there is of power in sound
> To breathe an elevated mood, by form
> Or image unprofaned; and I would stand
> Beneath some rock, listening to sounds that are
> The ghostly language of the ancient earth,
> Or make their dim abode in distant winds.
> Thence did I drink the visionary power.
>
> (II, 321)

What Wordsworth is impressed with here, and what he goes on to stress in the rest of the passage, is the indefinite and general character of the visionary or imaginative mood. Any form or image would profane it—that is, would hamper and constrain its godlike power by engaging it with concrete human life. Wordsworth prizes these "fleeting moods of shadowy exultation," as he calls them, just because they are shadowy rather than substantial. Thanks to them the soul

> Remembering how she felt, but what she felt
> Remembering not—retains an obscure sense
> Of possible sublimity, to which
> With growing faculties she doth aspire,
> With faculties still growing, feeling still
> That whatsoever point they gain they still
> Have something to pursue.
>
> (II, 335)

Because the soul remembers *how* she felt, but can't remember *what* she felt, she retains an obscure sense of sublimity as an undefined, unlimited possibility. To this goal of spiritual height and grandeur in general, the soul aspires with ever-growing faculties. But however far the faculties of the soul may reach, whatever concrete forms and images of sublimity the soul may realize itself in, the imagination still leads it on, revealing that it "still has something to pursue." Imagination marks out for the human soul an endless upward path, it leads it into infinity. Or as Wordsworth says about the growth of his own imagination at the end of *The Prelude*, it affords us

> The feeling of life endless, the one thought
> By which we live, infinity and God.
>
> (XIII, 183)

The Wordsworthian imagination doesn't come down from the mountaintop of vision with the tablets of a history in its hands. Not biblical, not Shakespearian, not even Miltonian, it has no story to tell. It is rather a metapsychological mood of shadowy exultation of the soul in which she catches glimpses of eternity. Because it is rapt beyond any specific imaginative content into empty upper cosmic regions, there is a strong touch of the negative, of the not-human, about the Words-worthian visionary power as it reveals itself to the poet in *The Prelude*, even though he is a poet to whom man is so dear. And this is the side of himself, the side of the visionary or imaginative rather than the human, on which Wordsworth lays unusual stress in middle age in defiant justification of himself as a still unrecognized monument of English poetry.

This separation of the imaginative from the human both-ered his good friend Crabb Robinson. On May 9, 1815, Robin-son noted the following in his diary:

> Wordsworth particularly recommended to me among his Poems of Imagination *Yew Trees* and a description of Night [*A Night-piece*]. These, he says, are among the best for the imaginative power displayed in them. I have since read them. They are fine, but I believe I do not understand in what their excellence con-sists. Wordsworth himself, as Hazlitt has well observed, has a

pride in deriving no aid from his subject. It is the mere power which he is conscious of exerting in which he delights, not the production of a work in which men rejoice on account of the sympathies and sensibilities it excites in them. Hence he does not much esteem his *Laodamia*, as it belongs to the inferior class of Poems Founded on the Affections. Yet in this, as in other pe-culiarities of Wordsworth, there is a *German* bent in his mind.[19]

Yew Trees and *A Night-piece* are passages of blank-verse medi-tation: one on ancient trees "produced too slowly ever to de-cay" which suggest thoughts about eternity and "Time the Shadow"; the other on the night sky which "the pensive trav-eller" casually looks up at with eyes that have been bent too much earthwards, to discover in the sudden splitting open of the clouds a vision of "immeasurably distant" stars wheeling away in the "unfathomable depth," a vision of infinity. The amount of human life in these poems is reduced—drastically reduced in *Night-piece*; they are poetry being stripped down almost to itself. Wordsworth in these pieces, as Robinson says, is interested less in the subject matter than in the power of the mind to exert itself imaginatively. About a wonderful sonnet of his, *With Ships the Sea Was Sprinkled Far and Nigh*, a masterpiece of light-hearted imagination gambolling with it-self, Wordsworth himself comments: "My mind wantons with grateful joy in the exercise of its own powers."[20] *Laodamia*, in contrast, a relatively late poem, is all about human desire; it is clamorous with human desire, the demand for human life, upon which demand the poet implacably, although remorse-fully, places his interdict.

Wordsworth, talking to Robinson, pronounces judgment on his poems uncompromisingly, without any sign of hesita-tion. But that is the middle-aged Wordsworth speaking, the champion of his own greatness. The young poet who wrote *A Night-piece* many years before, in 1798, did feel some hesita-tion; it shows up in the poem's final sentence:

> At length the vision closes; and the mind,
> Not undisturbed by the delight it feels,

Which slowly settles into peaceful calm,
Is left to muse upon the solemn scene.

He finds, the poet tells us, that his mind is "not undisturbed by the delight it feels." Although the double negative mitigates the disturbance, and although the delight the poet takes in the vision subsides into peaceful calm, the poet's mind is left musing—that is, in a state of meditative disturbance. What disturbs it is what disturbs us all as we look up at the night sky: no longer the tent or canopy of the heavens, enfolding us, in its modern mathematical infinity it is chillingly inhuman. Wordsworth's imaginative vision reaches out metaphysically to the immeasurable and the unfathomable; but the metaphysical, which is everything philosophically speaking, is nothing humanly speaking.

Although he vindicated himself as a poet of the sublime, of the visionary imagination, doubtfulness always dogged the idea of the imagination for Wordsworth, even when the imagination was engaged on its light and gayer side. This is illustrated, quite touchingly, by his companion poems about the Yarrow River and a passage concerning them in a letter. When he and his sister toured Scotland in 1803 he would not turn aside to visit the stream, much to his sister's regret—so the ebullient *Yarrow Unvisited* tells us. His reason:

"Be Yarrow stream unseen, unknown!
It must, or we shall rue it:
We have a vision of our own;
Ah! Why should we undo it?"

Eleven years later, in 1814, he saw the Yarrow and his vision of it was indeed undone, as the first stanza of *Yarrow Visited* declares.

And is this—Yarrow?—*This* the Stream
Of which my fancy cherished,
So faithfully, a waking dream?
An image that hath perished!

O that some Minstrel's harp were near,
To utter notes of gladness,
And chase this silence from the air,
That fills my heart with sadness!

But then the poet makes himself go to work; he labors man-
fully, against his own melancholy, and finds that after all
the Yarrow which had appeared so fair "to fond imagination," the Yarrow which was that power's "delicate *creation*,"
was matched and rivalled "in the light of day" by the actual
Yarrow:

But thou, that didst appear so fair
To fond imagination,
Dost rival in the light of day
Her delicate creation.

Even if the poem didn't show us, so honestly, the poet argu-
ing himself into feeling that his visit to the actual Yarrow had
been an occasion of joy, we would know that he is falsifying
his true feeling. His true feeling was a sense of dejection, of
loss—that fundamental sense of loss which overtook him in
maturity and which, all his creative life, was the other face
and profound negative of his sense of exuberant imaginative
power. We know this because he dares to say, right in the face
of his own *Immortality Ode*, that the actual Yarrow matched
and equalled the earlier Yarrow of his imagination *in the light
of day*. The light of day, the "light of common day," is exactly
what is "at enmity with joy" for him; the light of day is the
darkness of the prison-house which begins to close upon the
growing Boy; it is what causes the "vision splendid" which
still attends the Youth to fade away at last. The banal light of
day, gradually filling the glorious imaginative eye of our first
unthinking consciousness, puts it out, and with it the glory
and the dream, the radiance and the splendor. The light of
day darkens; but here in *Yarrow Visited* Wordsworth tries to
say, against his deepest sense of things, that it brightens.

Although Wordsworth worked hard over the second Yarrow poem and revised it repeatedly, he wasn't able to lift it up out of its inertness; he says this himself. Knowing that he had succeeded in the first poem, he had been "anxious that there should be no falling off" in the later one, he wrote on November 23, 1814; "but [such falling off] was unavoidable, perhaps from the subject, as imagination almost always transcends reality."* A poem about the actual Yarrow *must* be inferior to one about the imagined river—imagination beats reality almost any time. To "transcend" reality can mean something sublime and glorious, but with the littlest shift it means "enthusiastic" self-deception. *Yarrow Visited* betrays that shift. It calls the imagination "fond" (that is, foolish) and her creations "delicate" (that is, soap bubbles); the imagination is a dream and a delusion.

For Wordsworth in 1800, in the Preface to the *Lyrical Ballads*, the imagination didn't transcend nature; it dwelt with nature and bathed it with its light. Slowly, however, he was beginning to see that illumination as transcendence, as sublime creation. And that is how Wordsworth the critic, later on, defended himself in prose: as a great imaginative poet. But Wordsworth the poet, shocked by his brother's drowning, had already been speaking otherwise in 1805, in the Peele Castle poem (*Elegiac Stanzas*). There he turned against the imagination and called it "the light that never was on sea or land," "the Poet's dream," a "fond illusion"—which was what the solid, Miltonian-materialist Englishman in him always worried it was.† That was in the violence of his grief over his

---

*See Proust in *The Past Recaptured*: "So often, in the course of my life, reality had disappointed me because at the instant when my senses perceived it my imagination . . . could not apply itself to it in virtue of that ineluctable law which ordains that we can only imagine what is absent" (p. 133).

† But apt the Mind or Fancy is to rove
  Uncheckt, and of her roving is no end;
  Till warn'd, or by experience taught, she learn
  That not to know at large of things remote

brother's death at sea. In 1814, however, it is just a little Scottish stream that defeats him. In 1803 imagination beats reality, ambiguously (ambiguously, because the poet dare not accept the challenge of the real stream); in 1814 reality defeats imagination, unambiguously and in spite of all of Wordsworth's hard work.

Wordsworth's best and fullest account of the imagination is given poetically in *The Prelude*, not discursively in prefaces. In that poem the imagination discovers itself to the poet's conscious mind in little episodes of vision, or "spots of time" (XI, 257) as he calls them in English shockingly plain and unpretending. These episodes are quite ordinary and insignificant: he steals a boat as a boy, he hoots at owls, he stumbles on an old gallows. (Most of these things happened to Wordsworth in his boyhood.) But as these moments unfold in *The Prelude*, the whole scene is bathed and illuminated for him by the radiance of an unearthly significance; the ordinary earthly scene becomes unearthly, more than human. This unspeakable radiance and significance is literally unspeakable—the poet can't say what it means, only *that* it means, and means more than anything else. In all the "spots of time" the action of the imagination is an exhibiting of the imagination, a showing forth of unspeakable power and significance, out of the midst of ordinary human circumstances. We see in these moments how the content of Wordsworth's imagination is the imagination itself; how the subject matter of his poetry, in *The Prelude*, is the poetic power itself, the poetic power abstracted from any particular human object or concern and revealing in this way, even if only in flashes, its immeasurable reach.

From use, obscure or subtle, but to know
That which before us lies in daily life,
Is the prime Wisdom; what is more, is fume,
Or emptiness, or fond impertinence.

(*Par. Lost* VIII, 188)

Of course, there is another side to *The Prelude*, its autobiographical side. *The Prelude* is the story of how, as the title of Book VIII says, the "Love of Nature Leads to Love of Mankind." But this autobiographical story is unconvincing, weak. Wordsworth persuades you of his love of nature, God knows, but he doesn't persuade you that it leads to love of mankind, for which a few shepherds and beggars (solitaries and outcasts) must do duty in the poem. In his poem, life leads to poetry, not poetry to life. The love of nature leads Wordsworth to love of solitariness, to a love of poetry tending beyond mankind into pure or metaphysical imagination. And this is what makes *The Prelude* an early work of modern art*— that art which strives, with such grandeur, to know itself *as* art, in the misery of its Hamlet impotence as life.

The grandeur *and* the misery of modern art. There is no danger anymore of underrating the grandeur, the greatness. The great modern artists, stiffening into established figures, are now monuments. There is a danger of underrating the "misery," that is, modern art's feeling of life-separation, life-loss. What we find in the modern imagination is greatness of mind and poverty of nature. The result is a certain deathliness. This deathliness isn't something that modern art aims at; it isn't its wish, its death wish. It isn't betrayal of traditional

*"In turning his attention away from the subject matter of common experience, the [modern] poet or artist turns it in upon the medium of his own craft. The attention of poets like Rimbaud, Mallarmé, Valéry, Eluard, Pound, Hart Crane, Stevens, even Rilke and Yeats, appears to be centered on the effort to create poetry and on the 'moments' themselves of poetic conversion, rather than on the experience to be converted into poetry."—Clement Greenberg, *Art and Culture* (1961), 7.

Erich Kahler, writing about Thomas Mann's *Dr. Faustus,* puts it this way: "The traditional art forms have grown problematic through external evolution—that is, social and cultural evolution—as well as through internal evolution, evolution of artistic technique; art has become its own subject matter. And since the function of the artist . . . has been called into question by the moral and social events of our epoch, the artist himself is drawn into a kind of polyphonic soliloquy on his role in our world."—*The Orbit of Thomas Mann* (1969), 21.

values or perversity or elitism or failure of nerve, as used to be charged. The deathliness starts in the modern world, not in modern art; it belongs to the modern situation, and it is just the courage of modern art to express it. But neither is this pure, abstracted, life-separated character of modern art *not* misery, not deathliness, but a best thing which we should rejoice in, a summum bonum. The life-separation and life-reduction of modern art belong to the grandeur and misery of an epoch of profoundest transition, which in passing out of old knowledge of human life is unable to arrive at knowing human life anew, to arrive at a modern knowledge of what is truly human. Wordsworth's imagination isn't the least bit Byzantine, yet it is in danger of having no other "singing school but studying / Monuments of its own magnificence"— as Crabb Robinson felt.

The empty character of the Wordsworthian imagination— having for its subject matter only itself—this marked negativity, comes to crucial expression in that central and strangest and blankest moment of *The Prelude*, when Wordsworth describes how he crossed the Alps on his hiking tour through France in the summer of 1790. Leaving revolutionary France behind, Wordsworth and a friend were climbing the track which led across the Simplon and down into Italy, following some mule drivers because it was easy to lose the way in those days. All their effort was a straining upwards. At the noon halt they lingered awhile to catch their breath, letting the mule drivers go on; then they followed the track downwards to a little stream, on the other side of which the path seemed to continue up a high mountain. After a moment's doubt about the way, they chose the upward path and "climbed with eagerness," which turned into anxiety when they failed to overtake the mule drivers. But a peasant set them right: the path they were looking for led downwards with the stream, for *"we had crossed the Alps"*—so Wordsworth exclaims in the poem, with surprising emphasis.

Wordsworth prefaces this account by saying that though he passed a lot of his time while tramping in indulging a sentimental melancholy ("Dejection taken up for pleasure's sake"), his sterner and more vigorous side hadn't been put entirely to sleep. And this side of his nature was responsible for the "far different dejection," the "deep and genuine sadness" he fell into at the conclusion of the incident he has just related. For when it was finally borne in upon him that he had crossed the Alps, that the way was now down and not up, he fell into a depression. He did not interpret this feeling at the time. Let me try. I think that what depressed him was that his path, now all downhill, led ultimately back to England, where the twenty-year-old orphaned youth would have to face the necessity, about which his guardian relatives were always on his neck, of choosing a profession. Workaday life menaced him like an extinction, with its banality. Going to the Continent had put it out of his mind, but only while the walking tour pointed up and on; when it pointed back and down he became depressed.

Fourteen years later, however, when he was describing the episode in Book VI, imagination, snatching him up as if in a cloud, speaking to him in the accents of Sinai, revealed a much larger interpretation than the one I have just given of his fall of mood so long before. The interpretation is larger because it appears to Wordsworth in the light of his later life as a poet, and larger still because the personal revelation is at the same time a revelation of the modern spiritual destiny. The result of all of this is that the traveller's depression of years ago, becomes the exaltation of the poet now writing the poem in 1804:

> Imagination!—lifting up itself
> Before the eye and progress of my song
> Like an unfathered vapour, here that power,
> In all the might of its endowments, came
> Athwart me. I was lost as in a cloud,

Halted without a struggle to break through,
And now, recovering, to my soul I say
"I recognize thy glory." In such strength
Of usurpation, in such visitings
Of awful promise, when the light of sense
Goes out in flashes that have shewn to us
The invisible world, doth greatness make abode,
There harbours whether we be young or old.
Our destiny, our nature, and our home,
Is with infinitude—and only there;
With hope it is, hope that can never die,
Effort, and expectation, and desire,
And something evermore about to be.
The mind beneath such banners militant
Thinks not of spoils or trophies, nor of aught
That may attest its prowess, blest in thoughts
That are their own perfection and reward—
Strong in itself, and in the access of joy
Which hides it like the overflowing Nile.

(VI, 525)

This is a glorious passage. Although its effulgence might seem to obscure its sense, it is not unclear (only disconcerting). What is the imagination, as it reveals itself here? It is a "usurpation" of the workaday mind by a great "Power"—not only, mind you, of the ordinary working mind of common life, but also of Wordsworth's poetic mind working regularly every day on the "progress of his song." The usurpation is first felt as blindness and disorientation. There he is in his story on the crest of the Alps, with glittering air and light on every side, when imagination, like the rising mist catching a shepherd unawares on top of Helvellyn, issues from the fastnesses of his mind and stops the poet dead in his tracks—that is, in his story. *Imagination stops story.*[21] This first action of the imagination is purely negative and revives in some sort the depression he had originally felt in 1790 about feeling stopped in his life.

However, when the light of sense goes out as he is composing the poem in 1804, it goes out "in flashes," making momentarily visible to the mind that invisible world which, Wordsworth chants, is "our destiny, our nature, and our home." Home is a place where you can make yourself at home, not a mountaintop or a desert; the transcending of the material world would seem to promise us a substantial spiritual one. But what does the invisible world, here glimpsed, consist of? How is it furnished? With nothing real (realized), only with "possible sublimity" (II, 337). The militant imagination, taking off from the top of the world with a Miltonian-Newtonian rush of wings, arrives . . . nowhere at all. It wins no "spoils or trophies," discovers no God or Law of the World or Last Thing. It discovers (only) itself—the power to conceive unending possibility, the dizzying thought of cosmic infinity, onward-leading feelings of hope and desire, the expectation of something evermore *about* to be.

Thus the second action of the imagination is also negative, though in a complex sense. Wordsworth's negative sublime reflects the physics and the metaphysics and the aesthetics of an exploding age and an exploding universe whose superhuman immensities conceal ends it is impossible to descry. Such an age is unable to make out for itself the story it is in. Or rather, what is perhaps the same thing, it is unable to make *up* for itself a story to be in. It is the age of Shakespeare's Hamlet, who does not know what he should do, the part he should play, since he is unable to play the part assigned him by the old knowledge; of Pirandello's Six Characters who come looking for an Author to make up a story for them to play a part in; of Kafka's Land-surveyor K. in *The Castle*, who comes out of the cold looking for a job, a home, for a part to play in the story of us all.[22] *Hamlet* and *Six Characters in Search of an Author* and *The Castle* reflect the desperation of such an age; Wordsworth reflects its hope, militantly doing battle with the desperation.

What is disconcerting about the episode of Crossing the Alps is the apparent slightness, the pettiness in fact of the emotional experience Wordsworth had in 1790,* which when recollected in 1804 is sublimated beyond the heaven of heavens into "infinitude." When you first read the episode you don't understand what all the shouting is about. Wordsworth discovers he has crossed the Alps and suffers a letdown. A letdown! Out of this nothing, this contemptible, not vast, *nihil,* his imagination, godlike, creates an infinite world of spirit. What egotism, the egotism of a Jehovah, a creator God! Here under this aspect Wordsworth shows himself a son of Milton, who was a son of the Original Imagination of the Hebrew Bible and made so much of an apple's being eaten. Here, like Milton, he is a son who has no trouble becoming a Father of worlds. But under another aspect, the sublime spiritual world his imagination reveals is still tied to its humble psychological origins in being only a world of possibility, not an actual world. And here Wordsworth is no father of reality, but the disobedient Promethean son of possibility, a Hamlet child *moving about in worlds not realized,* as the *Immortality Ode* says— a Hamlet who rejoices at, not deplores in himself,

> those obstinate questionings
> Of sense and outward things,
> Fallings from us, vanishings;
> Blank misgivings of a Creature
> Moving about in worlds not realized,
> High instincts before which our mortal Nature
> Did tremble like a guilty Thing† surprised.

The modern artist, Wordsworth is saying here, is a creature of inwardness, full of obstinate questionings of sense and outward things, one who is haunted by a sense of fallings off and

---

*We recognize in this the poet of Simon Lee's swollen ankles, Alice Fell's duffle coat, of Lucy Gray and Goody Blake and Harry Gill and Peter Bell.

†*Hamlet* I.i.148.

vanishings away. But these *blank misgivings* which he feels are also *high instincts*, a mortal creature's sublime impulse to soar beyond mortality into *worlds not realized*—to the shock and consternation of our mortal nature. Wordsworth, as always, turns *Hamlet* upside down.* In the play, "erring" immortal being (the Ghost) starts fearfully before mortal nature reawakening; in Wordsworth, mortal nature does the fearful starting, at the awakening in itself of instincts so high as to reach beyond nature.

The revelation of the imagination to the imagination in Book VI of *The Prelude* is a mental event which interrupts the story Wordsworth is telling in 1804 about how he crossed the Alps in 1790. As befits modern revelations, Wordsworth describes the imagination as arising from below, "from the mind's abyss"—so the 1850 revision: "That awful Power rose from the mind's abyss / Like an unfathered vapour" (VI, 594). The mind is an abyss concealing awful power. But at the same time the revelation comes to him on a mountaintop, out of a cloud, in the old-time way. Wordsworth meets his imagination in the Alps as Moses meets God on Sinai, Moses finding the Divine and Wordsworth the "Faculty divine" ("the Vision and the Faculty divine" [*Exc.* I, 79]). Like the dream of the Arab fleeing before the flood to save the shell of poetry and the stone of science, the revelation he receives looks two ways: backwards to the biblical God, by its evocation of traditional feelings of sacredness; but also forwards to a modern ultimacy that is all promise and possibility, the power of the human imagination, rather than to that power realized in a concrete form. The word God in the mouth of the Wordsworth of the great years,

---

*Wordsworth always turns *Hamlet* upside down because he can't help but read Hamlet's passiveness as wise passiveness: "musing in solitude" was never anything but high endeavor in his eyes. More was needed, to be sure, "something must be *done*"—yet solitary musing for him was already doing a lot. (Both quoted phrases are from *Home at Grasmere*.)

whom Coleridge pronounced a semi-atheist, is always an equivocation because of this looking two ways.

Taking up his interrupted narrative, Wordsworth recounts how he soon shook off his mood of letdown and hurried with his companion down the path which they had missed, into a "gloomy pass." But again the narrative is interrupted, though not so obviously, by another passage of impassioned sublimity which describes how the poet is awed and deafened and exalted by the metaphysical thunder and lightning of Alpine nature:

> The immeasurable height
> Of woods decaying, never to be decayed,
> The stationary blasts of waterfalls,
> And everywhere along the hollow rent
> Winds thwarting winds, bewildered and forlorn,
> The torrents shooting from the clear blue sky,
> The rocks that muttered close upon our ears—
> Black drizzling crags that spake by the wayside
> As if a voice were in them—the sick sight
> And giddy prospect of the raving stream,
> The unfettered clouds and region of the heavens,
> Tumult and peace, the darkness and the light,
> Were all like workings of one mind, the features
> Of the same face, blossoms upon one tree;
> Characters of the great apocalypse,
> The types and symbols of eternity,
> Of first, and last, and midst, and without end.

(VI, 556)

No light of sense goes out here in flashes that reveal the invisible world. Here the light of sense brightens to such a point, illuminates so starkly the primary, primitive world of matter in all its bulk and power, as to make one cringe. But even as we cringe, the poet's hardy imagination, flying its "banners militant," is able to do battle with and wrest out of the antithetical material flux, the tumult and peace, darkness and light, a saving idea—the ever-changing yet ever-during things of the world of sense of Alpine nature are letters which spell out to the poet the great thought of permanency; they are "types and symbols of eternity."

"Fancy is given to quicken and to beguile the temporal part of our nature, Imagination to incite and to support the eternal." What Wordsworth experiences in writing about his tour of the Alps in Book VI is a two-part revelation of the "awful Power" of imagination. The theme of the first part is infinity. Here imagination's metaphysical power feeds on negativity by reading out of a feeling of dejection and desertion, on discovering the way no longer lay upwards, the soul's never-to-be-satisfied longing for, its destiny with a modern cosmic "infinitude," with an ever-to-be-realized something beyond all present things. The theme of the second part is eternity. Sublimity in the second passage is based on a substantial material presence rather than on the immateriality of the unrealized; indeed, it is based on material substance itself; it is an example of what Keats (to call on him again) named the "material sublime." Yet it is still negative (in an ordinary human sense) in that the primary world of matter of the Simplon Pass in which Wordsworth's imagination discovers eternity, is far removed from the common life of human beings.

From the Alpine heights of the sublime, Wordsworth drops down to the shores of Lake Como, into the human world of the beautiful, of gardens full of fruits and flowers and pathways roofed with vines, of dark-eyed girls:

> Como thou—a treasure by the earth
> Kept to itself, a darling bosomed up
> In Abyssinian privacy.
>
> (VI, 590)

This passage from above to below had archetypal force for him in his life. It figured to him the way of his imagination, the path marked out for him as a poet. The "awful Power" appears to him out of a cloud of darkness and makes him one of hers. But it is not his part, it is not a human part, to stay up there on the heights, much as Wordsworth might have wished; he must go down among the habitations of men—like a stream born high up in cavernous darkness which courses turbulently down to the plain below, there to become a quiet-flowing river "reflecting in its solemn breast / The works of man, and face of human life." This figure appears more than once in his work; at the end of *The Prelude* it is used to summarize his entire "poem on the growth of my own mind" (as he called the work):

> This faculty hath been the moving soul
> Of our long labour: we have traced the stream
> From darkness, and the very place of birth
> In its blind cavern, whence is faintly heard
> The sound of waters; followed it to light
> And open day, accompanied its course
> Among the ways of Nature, afterwards
> Lost sight of it bewildered and engulphed,
> Then given it greeting as it rose once more
> With strength, reflecting in its solemn breast
> The works of man, and face of human life;
> And lastly, from its progress have we drawn
> The feeling of life endless, the one thought
> By which we live, infinity and God.

(XIII, 171)

Wordsworth wrote this in middle age, in 1805. But the opposition of the militant-sublime-divine and the quiet-beautiful-human is already present in the experience as he describes it in its first freshness, in a letter written to Dorothy from the Continent in September 1790:

> It was impossible not to contrast that repose, that complacency of Spirit, produced by those lovely scenes [at Como], with the sensations I had experienced two or three days before, in passing the Alps. At the lake of Como my mind ran thro a thousand dreams of happiness which might be enjoyed upon its banks, if

heightened by conversation and the exercise of the social affections. Among the more awful scenes of the Alps, I had not a
thought of man, or a single created being; my whole soul was
turned to him who produced the terrible majesty before me.

On one side the "terrible majesty" of the Alps, on the other
man and the social affections; on one side eternity, infinity,
God, on the other the daily sensual life of men; and very early
he began to see it as his business to join the sublimity of the
one with the humanity of the other.

When Wordsworth ends the account of his Alpine tour, he
has a "parting word" for us; he didn't, he says, praise the magnificence of the Alpine region so as to depreciate other places,
feel rich there so as to feel poor everywhere else, "as if the
mind / Itself were nothing, a mean pensioner / On outward
forms." The imagination, no mean pensioner, is able to exercise its power out of itself, out of pure mind; it is no less po-
tent in the lowly plains than on the heights, so that exalted
grandeurs and near sympathies flow together into a single
stream of life. All of Wordsworth's experiences of Alpine majesty "administered"

> To grandeur and to tenderness—to the one
> Directly, but to tender thoughts by means
> Less often instantaneous in effect—
> Conducted me to these along a path
> Which, in the main, was more circuitous.
>
> (VI, 676)

But the qualification here, the admission if I may call it that, is
significant and applies not only to Book VI but also to the work
as a whole. The note *The Prelude* strikes is one of grandeur;
the impression it makes on the reader is solemn to the point
of being forbidding. The poem departs from loftiness only by
falling down from it, into flatness and (less often) uncouthness (as in the mock-heroic jocularity of the card-playing in
Book II, or the sarcasm about the child prig produced by

modern education in Book V). As for "tender thoughts"—
they are much less evident in the poem, except here and
there, and make an appearance by a circuitous path when
they make an appearance at all.

But after all it's not surprising that the keynote of *The Prelude*
is sublimity; its subject is the power of the imagination, did he
possess it?—and Wordsworth's first study of its workings in
his mind showed it as a mighty force. Uniting that force with
"the social affections," with "tender thoughts"; "reflecting"
with that awful power "the works of man and face of human
life"—this was the job of "The Recluse," the job to come, the
epic goal of Wordsworth's life.

The middle-aged poet, smarting under criticism, emphasized
one-sidedly the sublimity of his verse, in defiance of all those
critics and readers who saw him as a writer besotted with
creeping, piddling themes, idiots and daffodils and girls who
couldn't count. Yet all along the idea of sublimity never lost its
anxious side for him. The easy commerce (relatively speaking!) between above and below which was possible for a Hebrew prophet, a Homer, a Milton was not for him, a modern
poet. The danger of sublimity was the danger of fancying that
he felt "Divinity within him breeding wings / Wherewith to
scorn the earth," the solid seat of earth. Early in his career
Wordsworth laid down a kind of program for his poetry,
which was to humanize the inhuman, to soften sublimity and
make it tender, near. This was at the same time a program for
the poet and for his poetry; there was no distinction for him
between the two.

One of Wordsworth's many formulas for this program is
striking (he glances at it in the quotation from *The Prelude*
given just above)—"Union of Tenderness and Imagination."
It comes to us under interesting circumstances—not from
Wordsworth directly but from a letter of Charles Lamb's (February 15, 1801) in which Lamb quotes the phrase from a letter

Wordsworth had written him. (Wordsworth's letter is unrecovered.) Lamb was an exasperated admirer of the poet and quite funny in his exasperation, as we have seen. He begins by telling his correspondent that he, Lamb, needs to watch his pen in the future when expressing an opinion about the *Lyrical Ballads* to their author. Wordsworth had recently sent him a copy of the second edition, accompanied by an apology for not acknowledging sooner his receipt of Lamb's tragedy *John Woodvil*, his excuse being his "almost insurmountable aversion" to letter writing.

> This letter I answered in due form and time, and enumerated several of the passages which had most affected me, adding, unfortunately, that no single piece had moved me so forcibly as the Ancient Marinere, the Mad Mother, or the Lines at Tintern Abbey. The Post did not sleep a moment. I received almost instantaneously a long letter of four sweating pages from my *reluctant Letterwriter*, the purport of which was, that he was sorry his 2d vol. had not given me more pleasure (Devil a hint did I give that it had *not pleased me*) and "was compelled to wish that my range of *Sensibility* was more extended, being obliged to believe that I should receive large influxes of happiness & happy Thoughts" (I suppose from the L.B.) With a deal of stuff about a certain "*Union of Tenderness & Imagination*," which in the sense he used Imag. was not the characteristic of Shakesp. but which Milton possessed in a degree far exceeding other Poets: which *Union*, as the highest species of Poetry, and chiefly deserving that name, He was most proud to aspire to—then illustrating the said Union by two quotations from [*Michael* and *The Brothers*]. You see both these are good Poetry: but after one has been reading Shaksp. twenty of the best years of one's life, to have a fellow start up, and prate about some unknown quality, which Shakspere possess'd in a degree inferior to Milton and somebody else!!

What the "fellow" wrote to Lamb in 1801 anticipates the ideas we have already seen Wordsworth expressing in later years to Crabb Robinson, to Lamb himself, and to the public in the Preface and the Essay Supplementary to the Preface of his *Poems* of 1815; in these ideas he opposes his "poetical" or sublime imagination to the "human" imagination—"enthusiastic and meditative Imagination . . . as contradistinguished from human and dramatic Imagination." Yet in making this distinction it was never Wordsworth's intention to give up on the human. His aim as a poet was, just precisely, to unite "tenderness" (that is, imagination of the human) with imagination of the beyond-the-human. However, Wordsworthian tenderness is not the Shakespearian dramatic pathos of men and women acting and suffering in the drama of life; his kind of meditative pathos, as he said, has "its seat in the depths of reason, to which the mind cannot sink gently of itself, but to which it must descend by treading the steps of thought." Wordsworth names Milton as a precedent for his program of a poetry both tender and sublime. What he has in mind is the combination of grandeur and "lowliness" in that high-thinking poet: *Paradise Lost* commands a vast epic scene, an important part of which is nevertheless domestic and concerns a married couple and their orchard. Yet Milton is not at all domestic, small, tender. He is tender only in idea or in occasional touches. The conjugality of Adam and Eve is at the heart of his story, and yet that conjugality is a notorious example of the human flattened and extinguished under the weight of a sublime style and temper.

So Wordsworth's reference to Milton is not really illuminating. Nor are his references to *Michael* and *The Brothers*. These are both good poems, as Lamb says, and saturated with a tender humanity. But are they Miltonic, sublime—*imaginative* as Wordsworth means imaginative? They are not: they don't have that reach. Wordsworth's blank verse in these poems is portentous, as his blank verse always tends to be, but without in fact containing any portents. In their plainspoken realism they seem much more biblical than Miltonic; yet not biblical either but Bible-ish.

I can think of better examples of the "Union of Tenderness & Imagination" than Wordsworth gave Lamb—*The Ruined Cottage*, for one. Its pitifulness is as withering as fire; at the end of the poem we are carried beyond "the passing shews of being," all the pain of human life, into the mysterious region of an undefined consolatory eternity. Wordsworth's occasional poetry is full of such examples, once so familiar when Wordsworth was a household poet (when there was poetry in the household). The Lucy poems are such. But Tenderness-plus-Imagination does *not* describe the Wordsworth of his biggest effort, *The Prelude*. Like Milton, he is tender only in touches in his long poem; but unlike Milton his poetry *abounds* in examples of the tender sublime, which yet remain "touches" in the sense that Wordsworth didn't have a great story or epic design in which tenderness would have had its place. Milton had a story but little tenderness, Wordsworth lots of tenderness but only little stories.

But let me quote from a less well known poem of Wordsworth's which vividly illustrates this kind of Wordsworthian greatness. *The Affliction of Margaret* is a mother's lament over her missing son. It pitches us with shocking abruptness into the woman's huge grief:

I

Where art thou, my beloved Son,
Where art thou, worse to me than dead?
Oh find me, prosperous or undone!
Or, if thy grave be now thy bed,
Why am I ignorant of the same
That I may rest; and neither blame
Nor sorrow may attend thy name?

II

Seven years, alas! to have received
No tidings of an only child;

To have despaired, have hoped, believed,
And been for evermore beguiled,
Sometimes with thoughts of very bliss!
I catch at them and then I miss;
Was ever darkness like to this?

In the next several stanzas Margaret rehearses her history: how she sent her son out into the world "ingenuous, innocent, and bold"; how he may have done things that "wanted grace," as people said, but never anything base to make her blush. (But this starts thoughts in the reader's head.) She suffered from the thought that he was simply neglecting her; and "being blind," she called on pride to defend her against the charge which might be implied by her son's neglect, saying she had been a kind mother, "as kind as ever breathed." But her tears have drowned her pride. The poem is about Margaret's "affliction," her torturing uncertainty, her grief; it is not a "story" about a lost son.

Continuing through the latter stanzas, the poem broadens out into an expression of cosmic anguish and fear, each stanza ending in a triplet which rises into a cry, or declines pitifully, or passes off into infinity—or which really does all of these things together.

VIII

Perhaps some dungeon hears thee groan,
Maimed, mangled by inhuman men;
Or thou upon a desert thrown
Inheritest the lion's den;
Or hast been summoned to the deep,
Thou, thou and all thy mates, to keep
An incommunicable sleep.

IX

I look for ghosts; but none will force
Their way to me: 'tis falsely said

That there was ever intercourse
Between the living and the dead;
For, surely, then I should have sight
Of him I wait for day and night,
With love and longings infinite.

X

My apprehensions come in crowds;
I dread the rustling of the grass;
The very shadows of the clouds
Have power to shake me as they pass:
I question things and do not find
One that will answer to my mind;
And all the world appears unkind.

XI

Beyond participation lie
My troubles, and beyond relief:
If any chance to heave a sigh,
They pity me, and not my grief.
Then come to me, my Son, or send
Some tidings that my woes may end;
I have no other earthly friend!

The mother's human emotion reaches out into the infinity of
the deep, into the eternity of "incommunicable sleep." Her
"love and longings" are "infinite" in more than the conven-
tional sense of such a phrase, in that they *seek* the infinite; and
in reaching so far out they become uncanny, beyond-the-
human, sublime. Margaret is a little human point whose fear
broadens out through the rustling grass around her, the shadows of the clouds above her, into the cosmos; the broad cosmos, structured by her sublime grief, bears down (I think of
an upended triangle) on the little human point of the mother.
"If any chance to heave a sigh," she says with Wordsworthian
profundity in the last stanza, "They pity *me*, and not my
grief." They pity the human being, but because her grief
strains beyond herself and human life to touch eternity, it is

"beyond participation" by others. Her grief has drawn her into an immense solitude.*

Epical and Elegiacal

Wordsworth thought of childhood as a time of "glad animal movements" (*Tintern Abbey*), of restless, wild activity, before we are "tamed and humbled down" by "custom" (*Prel.* V, 545). In the child, he saw the original human creature, the aboriginal father of the man. So it is fitting that he should compare himself at the age of five, running naked the whole summer long, to the naked aborigines of the American plains. He would splash all day in a mill race off the river which passed just behind his father's house in Cockermouth, or "course" the adjacent fields, or stand alone

> Beneath the sky, as if I had been born
> On Indian plains, and from my mother's hut
> Had run abroad in wantonness to sport
> A naked savage, in the thunder-shower.

> > (*Prel.* I, 301)

But it isn't only the child who runs abroad in wantonness; the grown-up poet does so too. In *Stanzas Written in My Pocket-copy of Thompson's Castle of Indolence*, Wordsworth imagines himself and Coleridge as dwellers in a paradisal castle where there is neither toiling nor spinning. They are happy *fainéants* "from earthly labour free," Coleridge being portrayed as a busy idler and himself, in the following lines, as a dreamy one:

> Within our happy Castle there dwelt One
> Whom without blame I may not overlook;

* "What is lonely," says Bradley in his great Oxford Lecture on Wordsworth, "is a spirit. To call a thing lonely or solitary is, with him, to say that it opens a bright or solemn vista into infinity."

For never sun on living creature shone
Who more devout enjoyment with us took:
Here on his hours he hung as on a book,
On his own time here would he float away,
As doth a fly upon a summer brook.

Yet there is some question about each one's right to be there:
Coleridge's forehead is noticeably "profound," he thinks too
much*; and about Wordsworth himself the poem goes on to
say that

    often would he leave our peaceful home
And find elsewhere his business or delight;
Out of our Valley's limits did he roam:
Full many a time, upon a stormy night,
His voice came to us from the neighbouring height;
Oft could we see him driving full in view
At mid-day when the sun was shining bright;
What ill was on him, what he had to do,
A mighty wonder bred among our quiet crew.

Ah! piteous sight it was to see this Man
When he came back to us, a withered flower,—
Or like a sinful creature, pale and wan.
Down would he sit; and without strength or power
Look at the common grass from hour to hour:
And oftentimes, how long I fear to say,
Where apple-trees in blossom made a bower,
Retired in that sunshiny shade he lay;
And, like a naked Indian, slept himself away.

What is the explanation for this restless driving up and
down, the description of whose aftermath suggests some
kind of debauch?

Some thought he was a lover, and did woo:
Some thought far worse of him, and judged him wrong;

---

*Wordsworth recurs to Coleridge's forehead (and eyes) in his memorial lines
(*Extempore Effusion*):
    The rapt One, of the godlike forehead,
    The heaven-eyed creature sleeps in earth.

But verse was what he had been wedded to;
And his own mind did like a tempest strong
Come to him thus, and drove the weary Wight along.

Poetry is the explanation, for "verse is what he had been wedded to." The poet drives abroad in solitude like a wild Indian,
like the little naked savage he had been at five; but now it is
not animal impulse, nature, which drives him but "his own
mind," working tempestlike. The effect of these tempestuous
mental exertions is wasting: the poet comes back to the castle
"a withered flower." Boy and man are wanton, wild, but the
man "wanton[s] in wild Poesy"—to quote from lines in the
last book of *The Prelude* in which Wordsworth recalls his and
Coleridge's first times together (XIII [1850], 420). For Wordsworth the imagination was wanton, which is to say a restless,
insubordinate power of the mind careless of "our Valley's limits," careless of law and limitation; although the law that is
being violated here is not the law of work of the unredeemed
world but the "law" of idleness of paradise—which is just
precisely the place where there are no laws, except the one
law against eating of the Tree of Knowledge. But that is just
the law the "sinful creature" breaks, by his hard-driving pursuit of the knowledge of the mind of man which is poetry. The
trouble in this Wordsworth paradise is poetry, the disturber of
the peace the poet.

Yet the poem ends on the note of repose rather than dis-
quiet, with the two friends easy in their Eden:

There did they dwell—from earthly labour free,
As happy spirits as were ever seen;
If but a bird, to keep them company,
Or butterfly sate down, they were, I ween,
As pleased as if the same had been a Maiden-queen.

In the first stanza Wordsworth describes himself as one than
whom nobody took "more devout enjoyment" in being idle;
his idleness is devotional, religious. But a militant impulse to
verse, working irrepressibly, keeps driving the poet abroad,

and the contented purposelessness of the paradise of nature is shattered by the striving imagination. The conflict between the two principles (if that is the right word) is drawn so sharply that you would think a showdown is in the making. Wordsworth, however, was no poet of showdowns, least of all of one between poetry and nature; there is no confrontation. But neither does he try to arbitrate or reconcile the issue. All that happens is that the poet (with his friend the thinker) is reestablished in the peace and quiet of the castle, with no more said.

Wordsworth shows the poet in the Castle of Indolence *Stanzas* as being like the child of nature of *The Prelude* in delighting in storms and solitudes and coursing about wantonly like an Indian. The suggestion which this analogy has for him is that nature and imagination share a fundamental principle of energy, that mind belongs with nature. There is no surprise in this, of course; his Wordsworthianism consisted precisely in discovering analogies between nature and man which, he hoped, were something more than metaphors or impositions of the mind. As the idea of the imagination as a *power*—and perhaps therefore an overweening power, a dangerous power reaching beyond nature and human nature—grew in his thought during the course of his association with Coleridge and the writing of *The Prelude*, the reassurance he got from the analogy became more necessary to him. "We Poets," he writes in *Resolution and Independence*,

> in our youth begin in gladness;
> But thereof come in the end despondency and madness

—and he didn't want that to happen to him. Yet that is the danger threatening the poet, for his movements aren't glad animal movements like the child's but violent mental ones; the heights and depths through which he ranges are perilous regions of the mind bordering on the unearthly. Wordsworth's saying in the *Stanzas* that the poet has been "wedded to" verse has the same aim as his joining boyhood and poethood through Indian-likeness: to draw poetry over to the side of nature and human nature by analogy. But here too the analogy is strictly limited. The poet's marriage to verse doesn't bring him "quiet days,"* but leads him rather into wasting solitudes of mental effort, expectation, and desire from which he returns "pale and wan" and "without strength or power."

Just as Wordsworth sees the grown-up poet as being like the boy in being Indian-like, in this way uniting militant spirituality with natural-spiritedness, so in *The Prelude* he sees the boy as being like the poet in owning powers of the imagination—there is more to childhood than glad *animal* movements. However, the boy's imagination is not the poet's self-conscious one which bends so ardently to nature just because it is separated from it. His is the primordial imaginative power of the race by which the child still lives in the first creating day that set the human world going, the power that is the very principle of human hope and effort. The poet's imagination also shares in that first power, but only weakly, as the *Immortality Ode* laments, for growing up has carried the poet far away from the glowing East. "Our childhood sits," writes Wordsworth (to quote again the wonderful passage in *The Prelude* apropos the tales and romances of his childhood reading),

> Our childhood sits,
> Our simple childhood, sits upon a throne
> That hath more power than all the elements.

He can't guess what this means about our human origins or about our future destiny,

> But so it is; and in that dubious hour,
> That twilight when we first begin to see
> This dawning earth, to recognize, expect—

---

* "Quiet days, fair issue, and long life" are what Ferdinand hopes for from his marriage to Miranda in *The Tempest* (IV.i.24).

And in the long probation that ensues,
The time of trial ere we learn to live
In reconcilement with our stinted powers,
To endure this state of meagre vassalage,
Unwilling to forego, confess, submit,
Uneasy and unsettled, yoke-fellows
To custom, mettlesome and not yet tamed
And humbled down—oh, then we feel, we feel,
We know, when we have friends. Ye dreamers, then,
Forgers of lawless tales, we bless you then—
Imposters, drivellers, dotards, as the ape
Philosophy will call you—then we feel
With what, and how great might ye are in league,
Who make our wish our power, our thought a deed,
An empire, a possession. Ye whom time
And seasons serve—all faculties—to whom
Earth crouches, th' elements are potter's clay,
Space like a heaven filled up with northern lights,
Here, nowhere, there, and everywhere at once.

(V, 531)

The explicit target of Wordsworth's anger here is the ape philosophy, decrying stories (*lawless* stories*), all that world of wonders, as lying fictions. Yet the deep anger of these lines has less to do with philosophy than with life, with life-loss, with the reducedness of life. Coleridge says somewhere that the key to Wordsworth is acquiescence. That is so; and just its being so explains the angry, rebellious outcry which these lines make against learning to live in reconcilement with stinted powers, in meager vassalage; foregoing, confessing, submitting; stooped beneath the yoke of custom, tamed and humbled down. Wordsworth thanks his sister at the end of *The Prelude* for softening his oversternness; he thanks Coleridge for helping him to chasten and stem the rapture of the hallelujah which he felt from all that breathes and is, so that

---

*Wordsworth tamed down *lawless* into *daring* in the 1850 version, thus acting out his own words.

due place might be given to the claims of duty and the truths of human suffering. But here he isn't thankful. In the *Immortality Ode* he refuses to grieve, finding strength instead in years that bring the philosophic mind. But here the thought of how much is lost, and so early, in vigor, power, vividness, vivacity, the thought of how much manhood is lost in becoming a man of the nineteenth century, causes him to cry out in unphilosophic anger against the exiguousness of the real, the given, the common, *das Gemeine*, and to uphold defiantly the imagination of the marvellous, which makes our wish our power, our thought a deed, which fills the blank void of the unrealized surrounding the given with wonders, with possible sublimities, as the northern lights fill the inane void of space, transforming it into a heaven.

The rebellion, the unusual anger, ends with the paragraph. In the next one, submitting to the yoke, dethroned and humbled, we pass over with Wordsworth "from our native continent / To earth and human life," where "we begin to love what we have seen; / And sober truth, experience, sympathy, / Take stronger hold of us." Wordsworth wrestled with his sense of loss all through his great decade. The thing lost is paradise, and about that he is of two minds. One mind is elegiacal, the other epical. In *Tintern Abbey*, elegiacal Wordsworth laments the loss of aching joys and dizzy raptures, but finds in traditional elegiacal fashion that "for such loss" there is "abundant recompense"—echoing with this phrase the "large recompense" awarded Lycidas for early death.* For the lost paradise of "thoughtless youth" Wordsworth is compensated with thoughtfulness, "the joy of elevated thoughts." In the *Immortality Ode* mind again, now called the philosophic mind, is his recompense for irretrievable loss.

Wordsworth's work is so generally elegiacal because he is a

---

* Now Lycidas, the shepherds weep no more;
Henceforth thou art the Genius of the shore,
In thy large recompense. . . .

memory poet, and for him memory is elegiacal in its essence.
The daffodils poem, for all the fluttering and dancing, twinkling and tossing, has a strong undertone of regret. Though
the poet's heart dances with the daffodils in the last line, they
are daffodils of the "inward eye," memorial daffodils of his
solitary "couch," not the ones actually seen in the earlier stanzas. And even the actual daffodils had been a "show," an
appearance—

> I gazed—and gazed—but little thought
> What wealth the show to me had brought

—and as such were withdrawn from him in their full substan-
tiality. The poet's solitary inward-dwellingness, sounded in
the profound violin strain of "I wandered lonely as a cloud"
(extraordinary line!), insubstantializes everything. For this
Spectator ab extra the daffodils lie, all of nature ultimately lies,
on the other side of a gulf of contemplation, not *in* him or he
in it. He lives out of the midst of life, on an accumulation of
"wealth" which starts to dwindle soon enough, telling over
his store of memories with a sort of miserliness.

The Prelude is elegiacal recollection for the most part, out of
which intermittently shine epical intimations of the "renova-
tion" of self and world. The poem begins on a high note of
heroic elation, Wordsworth proclaiming "The earth is all before me" (I, 15). All is, quite unusually, prospective in the introductory 271 lines; and looming largest for him in the prospect is his purpose to compose "a glorious work" (I, 158). But
doubts and anxieties assail him. Every hour his mind "Turns
recreant to her task" (I, 260); like a Hamlet he is paralyzed before the epic task,

> for either still I find
> Some imperfection in the chosen theme,
> Or see of absolute accomplishment
> Much wanting—so much wanting—in myself,

> That I recoil and droop, and seek repose
> In indolence from vain perplexity.
>
> (I, 263)

But in reproaching his recreant mind for its irresolution, he turns from the prospective to the retrospective:

> Was it for this
> That one, the fairest of all rivers, loved
> To blend his murmurs with my nurse's song,
> And from his alder shades and rocky falls,
> And from his fords and shallows, sent a voice
> That flowed along my dreams?
>
> (I, 272)

And a great work of modern poetry is launched, though not "a glorious [which is to say an epic] work."

Although *The Prelude* turns back to the past almost immediately, the note of elation continues to ring through the first two books about "Childhood and School-time." It is not now, however, the militant elation of *doing* of *The Prelude*'s introductory lines, of prospective great accomplishment, but an exultation of remembered *being*:

> with bliss ineffable
> I felt the sentiment of being spread
> O'er all that moves, and all that seemeth still,
> O'er all that, lost beyond the reach of thought
> And human knowledge, to the human eye
> Invisible, yet liveth to the heart,
> O'er all that leaps, and runs, and shouts, and sings,
> Or beats the gladsome air, o'er all that glides
> Beneath the wave, yea, in the wave itself
> And mighty depth of waters.
>
> (II, 419)

Then this exultation, this bliss, this "morning gladness" (VI, 63) starts to die away elegiacally as the suffocating weight of habitual life ("Heavy as frost, and deep almost as life!") presses down on the youth; the grown man finds that he can only "see by glimpses now, when age comes on, / May scarcely see at all" (XI, 337).

Looking back in Book III on the account of his youth which he gives in the first two books, the poet sees it as soul-history rather than life-history, "for my theme has been / What passed within me."

> Of genius, power,
> Creation and divinity itself,
> I have been speaking, for my theme has been
> What passed within me. Not of outward things
> Done visibly for other minds—words, signs,
> Symbols or actions—but of my own heart
> Have I been speaking, and my youthful mind.

Because the formation of the human heart and mind as he presents it is a revelation of "genius, power, / creation and divinity itself," he is struck with awe; it is a mighty theme, even though it is a theme of meditation and introspection rather than of action. Like Milton, Wordsworth finds his argument heroic, even though it is not the battle argument of a Homer or a Virgil.

> O heavens, how awful is the might of souls,
> And what they do within themselves while yet
> The yoke of earth is new to them, the world
> Nothing but a wild field where they were sown.
> This is, in truth, heroic argument,
> And genuine prowess. . . .

However, this epic poem of the soul, he quickly tells us before the sentence in which he announces it is out, is untellable:

> This is, in truth, heroic argument,
> And genuine prowess—which I wished to touch,

With hand however weak—but in the main
It lies far hidden from the reach of words.

(III, 171)

It is untellable for the most part. What part of it then *is* tell-
able, can be reached by words? The spots of time. In the spots
of time the sentiment of being, of the illimitable depth and
power of being of the soul, is renewed ("renovated"):

There is in our existence spots of time,
Which with a distinct preeminence retain
A renovating virtue, whence, depressed
By false opinion and contentious thought,
Or aught of heavier or more deadly weight
In trivial occupations and the round
Of ordinary intercourse, our minds
Are nourished and invisibly repaired.

This is expressed so modestly (not to say insipidly). Yet the
little spots of time aren't humble experiences at all; they lurk

Among those passages of life in which
We have the deepest feeling that the mind
Is lord and master, and that outward sense
Is but the obedient servant of her will.

(XI, 257)

The imagination is *not* modest. Working through humble episodes of sense, it reveals itself, by fitful illuminations, as a
power of dominion over sense.

As a poem about the power of the imagination, about recollection deepening into vision, *The Prelude* is more than elegiacal. But this occurs in "spots," spottily. What the imagination sees in these episodes is its power *to* see; it doesn't *with*
this power see a vision of the whole—which is to say a story
of the beginning, middle, and end of things. That is why *The
Prelude* lacks unity. *The Prelude* has a theme; Wordsworth sums
it up succinctly at the end of the poem—"the discipline / And

consummation of the poet's mind" (XIII, 270). But a theme is not a form. In its very first shape—the two-part *Prelude* of 1799—the poem was a relatively short one of 978 lines and had the character of an extended dithyramb, or hymn of recollection of the birth of imaginative power in the poet's life. Here is how Wordsworth himself remembered that first outpouring:

> I sang
> Aloud in dithyrambic fervour, deep
> But short-lived uproar, like a torrent sent
> Out of the bowels of a bursting cloud
> Down Scawfell or Blencathara's rugged sides,
> A waterspout from heaven.
>
> (Prel. VII, 4)

That original *Prelude* is the most satisfying one as regards its poetic form.[23] It all hangs more or less together as a prolonged effusion. But then Wordsworth added to it, inordinately; partly he was making up for his non-start with "The Recluse." Of course we shouldn't want *not* to have the monumental *Prelude*. But the longer it became the more of a hodge-podge it became—a great mass of poetic stuff the management of which cost him a lifetime of worrying over and fiddling with. The poem's uncertainty of form is evident in its clumsy transitions, in its general clumsiness. How the poem lumbers, between the dithyrambs and flights of exaltation! How crudely it *moves*! For it was never meant to be a poem of movement.

Wordsworth, understandably, didn't know what to make of this unprecedented work in which he talked at such unheard of, such embarrassing length about himself, didn't know, as a poet, what it was he had written, didn't know what to call it. That job fell to his wife after his death, who gave it the highly accurate non-title of *The Prelude*. Wordsworth was never sure about where the poem stood with respect to what he never stopped thinking of as his first business and main endeavor, "The Recluse." First he regarded it as an annex to his projected magnum opus, then its introduction. Then in the 1814 preface to *The Excursion* he separated *The Prelude* from "The Recluse" and called it a "preparatory poem" whose relation to the unwritten work he compared to that of "the ante-chapel . . . to the body of a gothic church." Having discovered a generous Gothic principle of form for his work, a principle which made room for an unfinished (not yet begun!) main structure, the now-unstoppable poet brings in his "minor pieces"* as well: when "properly arranged" these "will be found by the attentive Reader to have such connection with the main Work as may give them claim to be likened to the little cells, oratories, and sepulchral recesses, ordinarily included in" Gothic churches. Wordsworth has lost heart. By arranging all his poems "Gothically" so as to compose them into one great work, he is confessing his inability to compose a great work.†

The Prelude is passages. You don't sit down to it as to a narrative; you go to it for its passages, for its illuminations, for its intermittent thunder of great verse. In between the illuminations, writes Wordsworth (not in fact in *The Prelude* but in the peroration of *Home at Grasmere*),

> I mix more lowly matter; with the thing
> Contemplated, describe the Mind and Man
> Contemplating; and who, and what he was—
> The transitory Being that beheld
> The Vision; when and where, and how he lived.

(847)

The narrative side of *The Prelude*, the life story it tells, is "lowly matter"; the poem's visions are its sublime matter. Thus story and vision, life and mind remain divided, though in the passage from which the above is quoted, Wordsworth has just

---

*For Wordsworth, less than epic was "minor."

†The aim of Wordsworth's Table of Contents was to draw all his poems into a grand, unitary architecture of song, to achieve epicality as it were administratively. Today his Table of Contents, with its divisions that break up rather than bring out the natural shape of his work, just looks queer—and elderly.

epically proclaimed his great purpose to unite them. Vision in
The Prelude is not a vision of *things* but a vision of possibility,
of "possible sublimity." *The Prelude* is not itself a story, an
epic; it is about the hope of epic story.

Barren Silence

Immediately before Wordsworth launched out, at the end of
Home at Grasmere, on the epic invocation in which he proclaims the "high argument" of the monumental poem he was
girding himself to write, he said something absolutely fundamental about the man who was going to do the writing, about
the child who was the father of that man:

> While yet an innocent Little-one, with a heart
> That doubtless wanted not its tender moods,
> I breathed (for this I better recollect)
> Among wild appetites and blind desires,
> Motions of savage instinct my delight
> And exaltation. Nothing at that time
> So welcome, no temptation half so dear
> As that which urged me to a daring feat.
> Deep pools, tall trees, black chasms, and dizzy crags,
> And tottering towers; I loved to stand and read
> Their looks forbidding, read and disobey,
> Sometimes in act and evermore in thought.
> With impulses that scarcely were by these
> Surpassed in strength, I heard of danger, met
> Or sought with courage; enterprize forlorn
> By one, sole keeper of his own intent,
> Or by a resolute few who for the sake
> Of glory, fronted multitudes in arms.
> Yea to this hour I cannot read a Tale
> Of two brave Vessels matched in deadly fight
> And fighting to the death, but I am pleased
> More than a wise man ought to be. I wish,
> Fret, burn, and struggle, and in soul am there.

(703)

What happened to this creature of wild appetites and savage instincts, disobedient and rowdy, who delighted in danger and deadly fights? Nature tamed him—nature tamed the nature out of him:

> But me hath Nature tamed and bade to seek
> For other agitations or be calm,
> Hath dealt with me as with a turbulent stream—
> Some nursling of the mountains whom she leads
> Through quiet meadows after he has learnt
> His strength and had his triumph and his joy,
> His desperate course of tumult and of glee.
> That which in stealth by Nature was performed
> Hath Reason sanctioned. Her deliberate Voice
> Hath said, "Be mild and cleave to gentle things;
> Thy glory and thy happiness be there."
>
> (726)

In the *Immortality Ode* and in the passage about his childhood reading in Book V of *The Prelude*, Wordsworth says that custom tamed him, not nature; it is a defeat. But in Book XIII, where he says it was Dorothy's and Coleridge's influences that tamed him (Nature working through the one, Reason through the other), and even more so here in *Home at Grasmere*, his taming is a victory accomplished in the depths of things; the disarming his militant oversternness arms him for his program of militant quietism, of uniting human tenderness and sublime imagination, nature and mind. For after enjoining him to cling to gentle things, the voice of Reason promises him that nevertheless the ardor which had inflamed his infant heart, the thirst to meet his foes and beat them, to leap over limits and explore darkness—his disdain and *contempt* as well as his love and longing—"All shall survive." It is impossible for them to die:

> "Nor fear (though thou confide in me) a want
> Of aspirations that *have* been—of foes
> To wrestle with and victory to complete,

Bounds to be leapt, darkness to be explored.
All that inflamed thy infant heart—the love,
The longing, the contempt, the undaunted quest—
All shall survive, though changed their office, all
Shall live; it is not in their power to die."

(737)

Knowledge shall not be purchased by the loss of power, mind by loss of nature. As with Milton's Adam, so with Wordsworth's (Wordsworth's Adam being himself): "For contemplation hee and valour form'd." But Milton's Adam was formed to be a thinker *and* a soldier, now the one and now the other, passing back and forth between the study and the field. Wordsworth the New Adam, musing in solitude, making field and study one, means to exercise his valor *in* his contemplating, in his poetry. So he can say goodbye without regret to the thought of being a soldier, which had lain in his mind all through his youth (unless Napoleon should invade England, in which case he would act the soldier's part literally). And he can also say goodbye to that other hope of his, to write a martial epic:

Then farewell to the Warrior's schemes, farewell
The forwardness of Soul which looks that way
Upon a less incitement than the cause
Of Liberty endangered, and farewell
That other hope, long mine, the hope to fill
The heroic trumpet with the Muse's breath!
Yet in this peaceful Vale we will not spend
Unheard-of days, though loving peaceful thoughts.
A Voice shall speak, and what will be the Theme?

(745)

And then comes the great invocation which concludes *Home at Grasmere*, announcing the epic-philosophical theme of Man, Nature and Human Life that he means to "chant" in "The Recluse."

But that was as far as he ever got. The "greater Muse" to

whom he appealed remained mute. (So did his lesser muse, Coleridge.) The peroration of *Home at Grasmere* thus led nowhere, remaining what it was, not the beginning of an epic but the conclusion of some autobiographical verses. And after finishing *The Prelude* in 1805, Wordsworth had more than enough of those.

The confidence Wordsworth expresses in *Home at Grasmere*, that the militant spirit of his childhood could never die, proved mistaken. It lapsed along with his poetry-making power, for imagination and "forwardness of soul" were one in him. The early Wordsworth had exulted in "the hour of feeling":

> Love, now an universal birth,
> From heart to heart is stealing,
> From earth to man, from man to earth,
> —It is the hour of feeling.
>
> (To My Sister)

Feeling was the *action* of the living soul. But already in his early thirties there are signs of disaffection with feeling. Saturnine-tempered Wordsworth was never much for small talk, the ordinary discourse of friends and neighbours: "the low" for him had to be sanctified with "the lofty," as he says in Sonnet III of *Personal Talk*. However, when he says so flatly in Sonnet I, without starting at his own words,

> Better than such discourse doth silence long,
> Long, barren silence, square with my desire;
> To sit without emotion, hope or aim,
> In the loved presence of my cottage-fire

we feel the chill of a monumental apathy beginning to gather.

The freedom, the spontaneity, the turbulence of feelings and desires began to be an oppression to him, a *weight*. In his sonnet on the sonnet, we find him preferring its "scanty plot of ground" because he feels "the weight of too much liberty." In young Wordsworth the feeling heart had made the silent laws he chose to obey; middle-aged Wordsworth writes an

Ode to Duty. It turns out that, in spite of the threatening sound of the poem ("Stern Daughter of the Voice of God!"), the "submissiveness" he embraces is still of his own choosing;* it is a latitudinarian kind of duty—yet still duty, not desire:

> Me this unchartered freedom tires;
> I feel the weight of chance-desires:
> My hopes no more must change their name,
> I long for a repose that ever is the same.

That uncompromising last line is breathtaking, even magnificent; he longs to be a stone. Out of the countercall of duty, submission, necessity, middle-aged Wordsworth also made great verse, but this was a penultimate stage.

In the *Tintern Abbey* lines, it wasn't chance desires that oppressed Wordsworth, but *the weight of all this unintelligible world*. Communion with nature, "the sentiment of being," lifted that weight; he owed to it

> that blessed mood,
> In which the burthen of the mystery,
> In which the heavy and the weary weight
> Of all this unintelligible world
> Is lighten'd:—that serene and blessed mood,
> In which the affections gently lead us on,
> Until, the breath of this corporeal frame,
> And even the motion of our human blood
> Almost suspended, we are laid asleep
> In body, and become a living soul.

But the blessed mood was still only a *mood*, not only for him personally but for all of us historically. It passed. Today nature, far from being able to restore us and protect us as living souls, itself needs to be restored and protected. When the "mood" passed for Wordsworth, he didn't seek relief in tradi-

---

*Coleridge, in *To William Wordsworth*, describes Wordsworthian Duty as "chosen Laws controlling choice."

tional religion, even if the traditional expressions of piety appearing in his poetry make it seem so. His Anglicanism was never more than nominal. Against the heavy weight of the unintelligible world, the Wordsworth wearing along in years opposed his own heavy weight of a rocklike apathy.

Nature was power, her power speaking to his; and by the power of his imagination brooding dovelike he was able to reach her indestructible heart of peace; he was able to defeat the violence of change and death. That is why, at the end of *The Ruined Cottage*, all the despair he feels "from ruin and from change,"

> all the grief
> The passing shews of being leave behind,
> Appeared an idle dream that could not live
> Where meditation was.

That is why the cottage girl still counts seven, though two in the churchyard lie; why Lucy, though dead and stone still in the ground, "*whirls round* in earth's diurnal course" with such lively motion. That is why Wordsworth's marvellous old men, the Old Cumberland Beggar, the Old Man Travelling, the Leechgatherer, the Veteran, are "not all alive nor dead, / Nor all asleep." They are pitiful, but because they defeat death by the courage of their natural being they can never die. They die, but death only continues their being insensibly subdued to the eternal patience of nature.

Wordsworth emulated the stillness, the stonelikeness of his old men. But theirs was natural and inconscient, as that of simple beings in nature; the Old Man Travelling

> is by nature led
> To peace so perfect, that the young behold
> With envy, what the old man hardly feels.

His, however, was conscious, active, "wise"—while the blessed mood was on him. Once the mood was gone, his quietism turned stubborn and stony. Coleridge's poem *To*

William Wordsworth, which was composed immediately after Wordsworth finished reading him the completed *Prelude* in January 1807, recites with profound understanding the main themes of his friend's great work "On the Growth of an Individual Mind." One theme is social, the hope that the French Revolution engendered in "the general heart of human kind"; when that hope is "afflicted and struck down" by Jacobin tyranny, Coleridge chants, it is "summoned homeward" by Wordsworth from the social to the individual sphere,

> thenceforth calm and sure
> From the dread watch-tower of man's absolute self,
> With light unwaning on her eyes, to look
> Far on.

Yet the light of that hope also waned. And as it waned the tower of strength of self in Wordsworth proved less than absolute, proved blind stones. Coleridge's latter days were peaceful and talkative; nevertheless, he prayed in his *Epitaph* to find life at last in death, after many a toiling year of finding death in life. Through his death in life there still ran the thrill of pain. But Wordsworth, blind as stones, clung blindly to his conviction, his dogma, that he was "one of the happiest of men." He died from the feet up. Like the great god Poseidon in a little fable by Kafka, the greatest singer in English between Milton and ourselves turned to stone:

> Poseidon got tired of his seas. The trident fell from him. Unmoving he sat on a rocky coast and a gull, dazed by his presence, described wavering circles around his head.

NOTES

ABBREVIATIONS

BL   S. T. C., *Biographia Literaria*, eds. Engell and Bate, 2 vols., 1983.

CL   *Collected Letters of S. T. C.*, ed. Griggs, 6 vols., 1959–71.

F   S. T. C., *The Friend*, ed. Rooke, 2 vols., 1969.

MM   Mary Moorman, *William Wordsworth, a Biography*, 2 vols., 1957–65.

N   *Notebooks of S. T. C.*, ed. Coburn, 3 double vols., 1957–73.

PrW   *Prose Works of W. W.*, eds. Owen and Smyser, 3 vols., 1974.

PWW   *Poetical Works of W. W.*, eds. de Selincourt and Darbishire, 2nd ed., 1952–59.

SC   S. T. C., *Shakespearian Criticism*, ed. Raysor, 2 vols., 1960 (Everyman).

Quotations from *The Prelude* are from the Norton edition, eds. Wordsworth, Abrams, Gill (1979); and unless otherwise noted, from the 1805 version.

SAMUEL TAYLOR COLERIDGE: "A SMACK OF HAMLET"

1. *Table Talk*, June 24, 1827.
2. SC II, 181.
3. CL III, 489.
4. CL III, 476.
5. CL II, 782.
6. "On the Living Poets."
7. "My First Acquaintance with Poets."
8. "Mr. Coleridge," in *The Spirit of the Age.*
9. CL I, 125.
10. N 2.2557.
11. SC II, 155.
12. CL I, 123.
13. CL I, 127. Cf. Norman Fruman, *Coleridge, the Damaged Archangel* (1971), 60.
14. CL I, 34.
15. Cf. Thomas McFarland, *Coleridge and the Pantheist Tradition* (1969), 195.
16. CL I, 310.

17. Thomas De Quincey, *Recollections of the Lakes and the Lake Poets* (Penguin), 58.

18. CL I, 354.

19. CL III, 104.

20. CL I, 37.

21. I. A. Richards, *Coleridge and the Imagination* (Midland, 1960), 60.

22. "Trooper Silas Tompkyn Comberbacke," in *Abingdon Harvest*.

22a. Thomas Carlyle, *Selected Writings*, ed. Shelston (1971, Penguin), 316–17, 322.

23. Cf. Elizabeth Schneider, *Coleridge, Opium and Kubla Khan* (1953), 246.

24. CL I, 320.

25. N 2.2355.

26. BL II, 15.

27. Quoted in Fruman, 413.

28. BL I, 221.

29. McFarland, 27.

30. BL I, 85.

31. N 2.2375.

32. CL I, 279.

33. SC I, 34; II, 224.

34. *Bio. Liter.*, ed. Shawcross (Oxford, 1907), II, 260.

35. *Ibid.*, 261.

36. BL II, 147.

37. N 1.20.

38. Cf. Fruman, 3–9.

39. Patricia M. Adair, *The Waking Dream* (1968), 5.

40. N 1.1554.

41. Adair, 8.

42. "Goethe as the Sage," in *On Poetry and Poets*.

43. SC I, 35; II, 150, 152.

44. SC I, 34.

45. SC II, 173.

46. SC I, 36.

47. N 3.3935.

48. BL I, 89.

49. BL I, 252.

50. BL II, 240n.

51. SC II, 152.

52. CL II, 832.

53. SC II, 223.

54. SC I, 22.

55. SC II, 152, 224.

56. SC I, 34.

57. SC I, 35.

58. N 3.4012.

59. SC I, 29–30.

60. CL II, 928.

61. CL III, 344.

62. Cf. Stephen Booth, "On the Value of *Hamlet*," *Reinterpretations of Elizabethan Drama*, ed. Rabkin (1969), 157.

63. *Interpretation of Dreams* (Avon), 299.

64. F II, 16.

65. N 1.1718.

66. F II, 16–17.

67. N 2.2086.

68. CL III, 307.

69. CL I, 186.

70. N 1.31.

71. N 2.2091.

72. N 2.2398.

73. N 1.1832, 1833.

74. N 1.1770.

75. *Coleridge's Miscellaneous Criticism*, ed. Raysor (1936), 210.

76. N 2.3231.

77. BL II, 16.

78. N 2.2086.

79. CL II, 1005.

80. CL II, 1020.

81. N 2.2091.

82. CL VI, 730.

83. CL V, 239.

84. Quoted from the draft of the poem copied into a letter to Southey, Sept. 11, 1803 (CL II, 983).

85. Cf. Fruman, 388.

86. CL I, 280.

87. N 3.3304.

88. CL IV, 888.

89. N 3.3470 and note.

90. CL III, 437.

91. N 3.3304.

92. N 2.2556.

93. N 2.2600.

94. F I, 519.

95. René Wellek, *Kant in England* (1931), 139.

96. CL II, 668.

97. BL II, 26.

98. CL I, 557.

99. CL II, 810.

100. BL II, 26.

101. CL IV, 574.

102. CL I, 294.

103. CL II, 1034.

104. MM II, 19.

105. CL IV, 564.

106. CL IV, 574.

107. N 2.2712.

108. "On Poesy or Art," *Bio. Liter.* (Shawcross), II, 253.

109. BL I, 304.

110. "Freud's Position in the History of Modern Thought," in *Past Masters and Other Papers* (1933), 180.

111. BL I, 9.

112. BL II, 16.

113. BL II, 65.

114. I quote from the first (1798) version.

115. N 3.3295.

116. Introduction to Rachel Bespaloff, *On the Iliad* (1947).

WILLIAM WORDSWORTH: MILITANT QUIETIST

1. MM I, 223.

2. *Selected Writings*, 322.

3. *Henry Crabb Robinson on Books and Their Writers*, ed. Morley (1938), I, 73.

4. A. W. von Schlegel, *Lectures on Dramatic Art and Literature* (Bohn, 1846), 406.

5. SC I, 34.

6. *The Pedlar*, in Jonathan Wordsworth, *The Music of Humanity* (1969), 174, 176.

7. CL II, 1054.

8. "Additional Table Talk."

9. BL II, 150.
10. *Home at Grasmere*, ed. Darlington, The Cornell Wordsworth (1977) Ms. B, l. 249 (p. 52).
11. PWW IV, 463.
12. CL IV, 575.
13. CL II, 1013; BL II, 119.
14. MM I, 152, 153.
15. PrW II, 349.
16. PrW III, 47n.
17. *Henry Crabb Robinson . . .* I, 93.
18. *Prose Works of W. W.*, ed. Grosart (1876), III, 460.
19. *Henry Crabb Robinson . . .* I, 166.
20. To Lady Beaumont, May 21, 1807.
21. Cf. Geoffrey H. Hartman, *Wordsworth's Poetry, 1787–1814* (1964), 46.
22. Cf. Lionel Abel, "Hamlet Q.E.D.," in *Metatheatre* (1963); also, my own *Terror of Art: Kafka and Modern Literature* (1968).
23. Cf. Jonathan Wordsworth, "The Two-Part *Prelude* of 1799," in the Norton *Prelude*.

INDEX